The Butterfly Gardener's Guide

Claire Hagen Dole
EDITOR

Janet Marinelli
SERIES EDITOR

Sigrun Wolff Saphire
SENIOR EDITOR

Mark Tebbitt
SCIENCE EDITOR

Joni Blackburn
COPY EDITOR

Leah Kalotay
ART DIRECTOR

Elizabeth Peters
DIRECTOR OF
PUBLICATIONS

Steven Clemants
VICE-PRESIDENT,
SCIENCE &
PUBLICATIONS

Scot Medbury
PRESIDENT

Judith D. Zuk
PRESIDENT
EMERITUS

Elizabeth Scholtz
DIRECTOR EMERITUS

Handbook #175

Copyright © 2003, 2007 (with updated resources)
by Brooklyn Botanic Garden, Inc.

All-Region Guides, formerly *21st-Century Gardening Series,* are published three times a year at
1000 Washington Ave., Brooklyn, NY 11225.

Subscription included in Brooklyn Botanic Garden
subscriber membership dues ($35 per year;
$45 outside the United States).

ISBN 13: 978-1-889538-58-7
ISBN 10: 1-889538-58-2

Printed by OGP in China. Printed on recycled paper.

Cover: Monarch butterfly on aster. Above: Gray Hairstreak.

The Butterfly Gardener's Guide

Butterfly Families

Claire Hagen Dole

Have you ever stopped in the midst of your garden chores to watch a bright yellow swallowtail as it lands on a coneflower? If you approach slowly, you may be surprised at how close you can get to a feeding butterfly. With a hand lens, gaze at its compound eye, its overlapping wing scales, and its long proboscis, uncoiled like a soda straw to sip nectar.

Keep that hand lens at the ready. You'll discover a fascinating world within your butterfly garden: Watch a female butterfly as she lays eggs on the undersides of leaves, and marvel at the development of tiny caterpillars within the eggs during the next few days. Keep an eye out for gobbling caterpillars pausing to shed their too-tight skins, and jewellike chrysalides dangling from branches as the insects transform themselves into dazzling adult butterflies.

Like all living organisms, butterflies are classified within the Linnaean system. Thus, a Painted Lady (*Vanessa cardui*) belongs in the kingdom Animalia, phylum Arthropoda, class Insecta, order Lepidoptera, family Nymphalidae, genus *Vanessa*, and species *cardui*.

Butterflies and moths make up the order Lepidoptera, which means "scaly wings." There are nine times as many moths as butterflies, a remarkable fact considering that scientists have classified almost 20,000 species of butterflies worldwide. Most inhabit the tropics; about 700 species can be found in North America, north of Mexico. In addition, many tropical vagrants are occasionally spotted in Florida and the Southwest.

Opposite: Sleeping blue early in the morning.

What determines a butterfly's placement within one family? It may share family characteristics such as wing structure, behavior, or caterpillar host plants. For example, butterflies in the large family Nymphalidae are called brushfoots because they all have short, brushy forelegs. They also tend to be strong, fast fliers.

A good regional guidebook, with geographic range maps and a caterpillar host plant index, is invaluable in the field or in your garden. See "For More Information," on page III, for a few recommendations. Your own observations on behavior, such as wing posture while basking, will aid in identification and bring greater pleasure to your butterfly watching.

Swallowtails
FAMILY PAPILIONIDAE

Large, with wingspans of up to 5½ inches, and colorful, swallowtails glide into your garden seeking nectar from a wide variety of flowers. They often flutter their wings while feeding, perhaps as a means of keeping balance. Their hindwings have tails that distract predators into attacking the rear end rather than the much more vulnerable head.

Male swallowtails engage in puddling (sipping minerals from wet sand) and hilltopping (swooping over a ridge to investigate territory and seek mates). The caterpillars may resemble bird droppings or have fake eyespots behind the head. Many caterpillars have an osmeterium, a forked organ behind the head that emits a foul odor when the caterpillar is threatened. Most swallowtails overwinter as a ridged green or brown chrysalis attached to a tree or building with one strand of silk.

Black Swallowtail

Eastern Tiger Swallowtail

Black Swallowtail (*Papilio polyxenes*)

Distinctive Marks Male is larger, with wider yellow vertical band. Wingspan 3⅛ to 4½ inches.

Caterpillar Green with black horizontal bands and yellow spots. To 2 inches long.

Range East, South, Midwest

Habitat Gardens, open areas

Caterpillar Host Plants Parsley (*Petroselinum crispum*), dill (*Anethum graveolens*), wild carrot (*Daucus carota*)

Eastern Tiger Swallowtail (*Papilio glaucus*)

Distinctive Marks Some females can be dark: black with hindwing border of yellow and blue chevrons. Wingspan 3¼ to 5½ inches.

Caterpillar Early instars are small, with an irregular brown and white pattern; they resemble bird droppings. Later instars are to 2 inches long, smooth, green with fake eyespots and yellow band behind eyespots. They feed high in tree canopies.

Range East, Midwest

Habitat Openings in deciduous woods; gardens

Caterpillar Host Plants Ashes (*Fraxinus*), birches (*Betula*), black cherry (*Prunus serotina*), tulip tree (*Liriodendron tulipifera*)

Western Tiger Swallowtail (*Papilio rutulus*)

Distinctive Marks Similar to Eastern Tiger Swallowtail but smaller. Wingspan 2¾ to 4 inches.

Caterpillar Same as Eastern Tiger Swallowtail

Range West of the Rocky Mountains

Habitat Gardens, open woods near streams

Caterpillar Host Plants Willows (*Salix*), alders (*Alnus*), big-leaf maple (*Acer macrophyllum*)

Giant Swallowtail (*Papilio cresphontes*)

Distinctive Marks Underside of wing is mostly yellow. Wingspan 3⅜ to 5½ inches.

Giant Swallowtail

Caterpillar Smooth, brown and cream, resembles bird dropping. To 2½ inches.

Range East, South

Habitat Citrus groves, forest edges

Caterpillar Host Plants Prickly ash (*Zanthoxylum simulans*), citrus trees (*Citrus*)

Pipevine Swallowtail (*Battus philenor*)

Distinctive Marks Glossy, blue-black wings. Wingspan 2¾ to 5 inches.

Caterpillar Purplish black with black and red fleshy filaments. To 2 inches.

Range East, South, California coast

Habitat Gardens, woodland edges

Caterpillar Host Plants Pipevine or Dutchman's pipe (*Aristolochia*). Chemicals in pipevine make caterpillars and adults distasteful.

Zebra Swallowtail (*Eurytides marcellus*)

Distinctive Marks Black and white vertical stripes; extra-long tails. Wingspan 2½ to 4 inches.

Caterpillar Smooth, green with yellow horizontal bands and one black horizontal band. To 2 inches.

Range East

Habitat Open, moist woods

Caterpillar Host Plant Pawpaw (*Asimina triloba*)

Whites and Sulphurs
FAMILY PIERIDAE

These medium-size butterflies with wingspans from 1 to 3 inches can be found in gardens, fields, and disturbed areas. Whites, which may have greenish marbling on the undersides of their wings, lay eggs on mustards (*Brassica*). They are strong fliers but do not wander. The Cabbage White is the most common white.

Sulphurs, named for their yellow coloration, may disperse in large numbers in the fall—perhaps as a response to a sudden population boom. Both male and female sulphurs are avid puddlers. Their caterpillars feed on legumes, such as alfalfas (*Medicago*) and clovers (*Trifolium*). Widespread cultivation of alfalfa has allowed Clouded and Orange Sulphurs to expand their range, mate, and produce hybrids. Most whites and sulphurs overwinter as pupae.

WHITES

Cabbage White (*Pieris rapae*)

Distinctive Marks Gray wing tips; very common on the wing in early and late season. Wingspan 1¼ to 1⅞ inches.

Caterpillar Green with vertical yellow stripe. To ¾ inch long.

Range Widespread

Habitat Open areas, gardens, fields

Caterpillar Host Plants Mustards (*Brassica*), nasturtium (*Tropaeolum majus*), spider flower (*Cleome*)

Checkered White (*Pontia protodice*)

Distinctive Marks White with dark checkered pattern. Wingspan 1¼ to 1¾ inches.

Caterpillar Smooth, blue-green with black spots and yellow vertical stripes. To 1 inch long.

Range Widespread, less common in the East

Habitat Fields, disturbed areas

Caterpillar Host Plants Mustards (*Brassica*), including pepperweed (*Lepidium*)

Cabbage White

Clouded Sulphur

Falcate Orangetip (*Anthocharis midea*)

Distinctive Marks White with orange tips on forewings. Wingspan 1⅜ to 1½ inches.

Caterpillar Green with vertical orange stripes on back, vertical white stripes on sides. To ⅞ inch long.

Range Southeast

Habitat Woods, open areas

Caterpillar Host Plants Rock cress (*Arabis*), bitter cress (*Cardamine*)

Closely Related Species Sara Orangetip (*Anthocharis sara*) looks similar; found in West.

SULPHURS

Clouded Sulphur (*Colias philodice*)

Distinctive Marks Yellow with black border. Some females are off-white instead of yellow. Wingspan 1½ to 2¼ inches.

Caterpillar Green with vertical white bands on sides. To 1 inch long. Same as Orange Sulphur.

Range Widespread

Habitat Fields, suburbs

Caterpillar Host Plants Clovers (*Trifolium*), vetches (*Vicia*), alfalfas (*Medicago*)

Little Yellow (*Eurema lisa*)

Distinctive Marks Bright yellow with black border. Wingspan 1 to 1½ inches.

Caterpillar Green with vertical white stripes on sides, downy. To ¾ inch long.

Range Very common in South; emigrates north in summer

Habitat Gardens, disturbed areas

Caterpillar Host Plants *Senna*, clovers (*Trifolium*), partridge pea (*Chamaecrista*)

Orange Sulphur (*Colias eurytheme*)

Distinctive Marks Yellow-orange with black border. Wingspan 2 to 2¾ inches.

Caterpillar Same as Clouded Sulphur.

Range Widespread

Habitat Fields, gardens

Caterpillar Host Plants Alfalfas (*Medicago*), clovers (*Trifolium*), many other legumes

Coppers, Blues, and Hairstreaks
FAMILY LYCAENIDAE

Known as gossamer wings, the butterflies in this family are tiny, with wingspans from ⅞ to 2 inches, and have iridescent wings. As color distinctions can blur, a field guide is useful: There is a blue copper, and many female blues are coppery in hue. Hairstreaks are named for a hairlike tail on each hindwing. Near the tail they often have an eyespot, creating the impression of a head with antennae. They rub their hindwings together to confuse predators into attacking this end. All rest with their wings closed.

Tiny, sluglike caterpillars of blues and hairstreaks may associate with ants, which protect them in exchange for protein-rich secretions. They often pupate in leaf litter and may spend the winter in this stage. Localized populations of some blues, such as the 'Karner' Melissa Blue, are vulnerable to habitat loss.

COPPERS

American Copper (*Lycaena phlaeas*)

Distinctive Marks Red-orange forewings with dark violet spots and edges; hindwings are violet with red-orange edges. Wingspan 1 to 1⅜ inches.

Caterpillar Light green or red, thick body. To ½ inch long.

Range East, western mountains

Habitat Disturbed areas, fields

Caterpillar Host Plants Dock or sorrel (*Rumex*)

BLUES

Eastern Tailed-Blue (*Everes comyntas*)

Distinctive Marks Fine tails on hindwings. Female is mostly brown. Wingspan ¾ to 1⅛ inches.

Caterpillar Dark green, with black vertical stripe on back, white and red stripes on sides. To ½ inch long. Overwinters inside seedpod.

Range East, Midwest, South

Habitat Suburbs, disturbed areas

Caterpillar Host Plants Clovers (*Trifolium*),

Eastern Tailed-Blue

Spring Azure

lupines (*Lupinus*), vetches (*Vicia*)

Closely Related Species Western Tailed-Blue (*Everes amyntula*). Wing underside is whiter, with smaller orange spot on hindwing.

Spring Azure (*Celastrina ladon*)

Distinctive Marks Early blue; avid puddler. Female has brown wing edges. Wingspan to 1¼ inches.

Caterpillar Smooth, variable color: green, cream, or rose. To ½ inch long. Feeds on flowers and buds of host plants.

Range Widespread

Habitat Wood clearings, suburbs

Caterpillar Host Plants Dogwoods (*Cornus*), *Viburnum,* blueberries (*Vaccinium*)

HAIRSTREAKS

Brown Elfin (*Callophrys augustinus*)

Distinctive Marks Brown, with hooked hindwings instead of tails; wing undersides are reddish-brown. Wingspan ⅞ to 1⅛ inches.

Caterpillar Green with red and yellow bands. To ½ inch long. Feeds on flowers and buds of host plants.

Range East, Great Lakes, West

Habitat Acid-soil woodlands, suburbs

Caterpillar Host Plants Blueberries (*Vaccinium*), azaleas (*Rhododendron*)

Gray Hairstreak (*Strymon melinus*)

Distinctive Marks Brown and gray with orange spot near fine hindwing tail. Female is browner than male; quick, low flier. Wingspan 1 to 1¼ inches.

Caterpillar Smooth, segmented, with variable color: green, cream, or rose. To ⅝ inch long. Feeds on flowers and fruit of host plants.

Range Widespread

Habitat Suburbs, disturbed areas

Caterpillar Host Plants Many, but prefers legumes and mallows (*Malva*)

Brushfooted Butterflies
FAMILY NYMPHALIDAE

Members of this large, diverse family that includes longwings, fritillaries, true brush-foots, admirals, satyrs, and milkweed butterflies were named for their short, brushlike forelegs—which makes them appear to have only four legs. Mostly medium-size (wingspans from 1½ to 3¾ inches), brushfoots have wings that are often partly orange. They may have cryptic markings on their undersides to camouflage against tree bark or soil. Brushfoots are strong, fast fliers. Some, most notably the Monarch, migrate long distances in spring and fall.

Many brushfoot caterpillars are covered with wicked barbs, which protect them from predators and parasitic wasps. They may feed in groups for safety, or rest during the day and feed at night. The chrysalides are often angled and knobby, with clearly defined wing shapes. They hang from branches, without silken girdles.

Longwings and Fritillaries

Longwings, or heliconians, are tropical butterflies with long, narrow wings. They have wingspans of 2½ to 3¾ inches. All use passion flowers (*Passiflora*) as host plants—a diet that renders caterpillars and adults distasteful to predators.

Fritillaries inhabit northern and alpine regions. Bright orange with a checkered pattern, they range in size from small to large (wingspans from 1½ to 3¾ inches), with most falling in the middle. Violets (*Viola*) are their primary caterpillar host plants. Greater fritillaries, such as the Great Spangled Fritillary, are also called silverspots, for the silvery markings on the wing undersides. Misnamed for its orange coloration, the Gulf Fritillary is actually a longwing.

Gulf Fritillary

Great Spangled Fritillary

LONGWINGS

Gulf Fritillary (*Agraulis vanillae*)

Distinctive Marks Black lines on orange wings. Flies with shallow wingbeats. Wingspan 2½ to 3 inches.

Caterpillar Black with dark red vertical stripes, branched spines. To 1½ inches long.

Range South, Midwest

Habitat Open areas, gardens

Caterpillar Host Plant Passion flowers (*Passiflora*)

Zebra Heliconian (*Heliconius charitonius*)

Distinctive Marks Black with yellow horizontal bands; slow, feeble flyer. Wingspan 3 to 3½ inches

Caterpillar White with small black spots and long, branched black spines. To 1½ inches long.

Range South

Habitat Forest edges

Caterpillar Host Plants Passion flowers (*Passiflora*)

FRITILLARIES

Great Spangled Fritillary (*Speyeria cybele*)

Distinctive Marks Large fritillary with black chevrons and dots on orange wings. Silver spots on undersides of hindwings. Wingspan 2½ to 3 inches.

Caterpillar Black with branched orange spines. To 1¾ inches long.

Range North, Midwest

Habitat Open areas

Caterpillar Host Plants Violets (*Viola*)

True Brushfoots

Some of our most familiar garden butterflies fall into this category. Painted Ladies, Red Admirals, and California Tortoiseshells often disperse from the Southwest in great numbers in late spring. Buckeyes spread north in summer, then migrate south in the fall.

Anglewings and tortoiseshells overwinter as adults in northern climes. Because of their long life spans, they need additional nutrients and seek minerals and amino acids from rotting fruit, tree sap, animal scat, and carrion.

Common Buckeye (*Junonia coenia*)

Distinctive Marks Brown with large eyespots. Iridescent, green overtones. Wingspan 2 to 2½ inches.

Caterpillar Black with orange spots, branched spines that are blue at the base. To 1½ inches long.

Range Widespread

Habitat Open, weedy areas

Caterpillar Host Plants Plantains (*Plantago*), snapdragons (*Antirrhinum*)

Mourning Cloak (*Nymphalis antiopa*)

Distinctive Marks Large, purplish-brown tortoiseshell. Wing undersides resemble bark; glides in flight. Wingspan 3 to 3½ inches.

Caterpillar Black with red spots; branched spines. To 2½ inches long.

Range Widespread

Habitat Open woods, suburbs

Caterpillar Host Plants Willows (*Salix*), birches (*Betula*), elms (*Ulmus*)

Mourning Cloak

Question Mark

Painted Lady (*Vanessa cardui*)

Distinctive Marks Mottled orange markings on brown; white bar at wingtip. Wingspan 2 to 2½ inches.

Caterpillar Variable: gray, purple, or yellow-green with yellow stripe on side, branched spines. To 1½ inches long.

Habitat Open areas, gardens

Caterpillar Host Plants Many, but prefers thistles (*Cirsium*)

Closely Related Species American Lady (*Vanessa virginiensis*), a widespread butterfly whose caterpillar feeds on cudweed (*Gnaphalium*) and everlasting (*Antennaria*); and West Coast Lady (*Vanessa annabella*), whose caterpillar feeds on mallows (*Malva, Sidalcea*)

Question Mark (*Polygonia interrogationis*)

Distinctive Marks Anglewing with brown spots on ragged orange wings. Underside resembles bark, with a silver hook on each hindwing. Wingspan 2¼ to 2¾ inches.

Caterpillar Black with vertical orange stripes and branched spines. To 1½ inches long.

Range East, Midwest

Habitat Open woods, suburbs

Caterpillar Host Plants Elms (*Ulmus*), hackberries (*Celtis*), nettles (*Urtica*)

Closely Related Species Eastern Comma (*Polygonia comma*), a butterfly whose caterpillar feeds on hops (*Humulus lupulus*) and nettles (*Urtica*).

Red Admiral (*Vanessa atalanta*)

Distinctive Marks Black with orange band. Not a true admiral, it is closely related to the Painted Lady. Rapid, zigzag flight; feeds on rotten fruit. Wingspan 2 to 2¾ inches.

Caterpillar Gray or black with branched white spines. To 1¼ inches long.

Range Widespread

Habitat Moist, open areas

Caterpillar Host Plants Nettles (*Urtica*)

Admirals

Medium in size, with wingspans from 2 to 3½ inches, admirals are attracted to tree sap and wet soil, but they will also visit garden flowers. Some gain protection from predators by mimicking unpalatable species: Viceroys look remarkably like Monarchs, and Red-Spotted Purples resemble Pipevine Swallowtails.

Tiny caterpillars overwinter inside a rolled-up leaf, attached to a tree with silk. In spring, they crawl out to feed on new foliage.

Lorquin's Admiral (*Limenitis lorquini*)

Distinctive Marks Black with white band and orange wingtip. In areas where their range overlaps, Lorquin's Admiral benefits from its resemblance to California Sister (*Adelpha bredowii*), a southwestern butterfly. Sister feeds on oak, making it unpalatable. Wingspan 2 to 2¾ inches.

Caterpillar Brown with white patch on back; bumpy. To 1¼ inches long.

Range West

Habitat Suburbs, moist clearings

Caterpillar Host Plants Willow (*Salix*), cherry (*Prunus*), apple (*Malus*)

Red-Spotted Admiral (*Limenitis arthemis*)

This is a relatively new term that applies to two subspecies, White Admiral and Red-Spotted Purple, which are described below. Despite their different colors, the two are considered subspecies of the same insect because they mate and produce fertile hybrid offspring.

White Admiral (*Limenitis arthemis* subsp. *arthemis*)

Distinctive Marks Black with white band. Hybridizes with Red-Spotted Purple, producing variable markings; attracted

White Admiral

Viceroy

to sap, rotten fruit. Wingspan 3 to 3½ inches.

Caterpillar Resembles bird dropping; brown and white with bumps on back; two branched horns behind head. To 1¼ inches long. Same as Red-Spotted Purple and Viceroy.

Range Northeast, Canada

Habitat Forest edges

Caterpillar Host Plants Birches (*Betula*), willows (*Salix*)

Red-Spotted Purple (*Limenitis arthemis* subsp. *astyanax*)

Distinctive Marks Resembles White Admiral but blue-black, without white band. Wingspan 3 to 3½ inches.

Caterpillar Same as White Admiral and Viceroy

Range East

Habitat Forest edges

Caterpillar Host Plants Willows (*Salix*), poplars (*Populus*), hawthorns (*Crataegus*)

Viceroy (*Limenitis archippus*)

Distinctive Marks Orange with black bands. Mimics Monarch; smaller with intersecting black band on hindwing. Wingspan 2⅝ to 3 inches.

Caterpillar Same as White Admiral and Red-Spotted Purple

Range Widespread, except in the West

Habitat Moist, open areas

Caterpillar Host Plants Willows (*Salix*), poplars (*Populus*)

Satyrs

Mostly medium-size, with wingspans from 1 to 2⅞ inches, satyrs are dull brown or gray, with several eyespots along the edges of their wings. They blend into their grassy habitat when basking with wings closed. Satyrs fly weakly near the ground and are more likely to seek tree sap than nectar.

The two-tailed caterpillars overwinter in leaf litter or attach themselves to grass blades with silk. In spring, they form smooth chrysalides on grass blades or in litter.

Common Ringlet
(*Coenonympha tullia*)

Distinctive Marks Pale orange, with small black spot on wingtip. Takes nectar from many flowers. Wingspan 1¼ to 1½ inches.

Caterpillar Green with yellow stripe on side, forked end. To 1 inch.

Range Northeast, West

Habitat Moist fields

Caterpillar Host Plants Grasses (*Poa, Stipa*)

Common Wood Nymph
(*Cercyonis pegala*)

Distinctive Marks Large, brown; may have yellow band over two eyespots on forewing. Variable; eyespots are larger on wing undersides. Wingspan 2 to 2⅞ inches.

Caterpillar Green with yellow stripes; red forked end, short red horns on head. To 1¼ inches long.

Range Widespread

Habitat Open areas, meadows

Caterpillar Host Plants Purple top (*Tridens flavus*) and other grasses (*Andropogon, Stipa*)

Common Wood Nymph

Monarch

Milkweed Butterflies

Of this tropical subfamily, the Monarch and Queen are the main North American butterflies. Their large orange wings spanning 3 to 4 inches warn predators that they taste bad, due to toxins they take up when feeding on their primary host plants, the milkweeds (*Asclepias*). They are strong fliers, undertaking long migrations in spring and fall.

Caterpillars are boldly striped in warning colors of yellow, black, and white. The rounded chrysalides, hanging from branches, are celadon-green with a band of gold dots. They become transparent, revealing the orange wings within, about a day before the butterflies emerge.

Monarch (*Danaus plexippus*)

Distinctive Marks Black veins are heavier on female; male has scent patches on hindwings. Wingspan 3½ to 4 inches.

Caterpillar White with yellow and black horizontal stripes, two pairs of fleshy filaments. To 2¾ inches long.

Range Widespread

Habitat Open areas, gardens

Caterpillar Host Plants Milkweeds (*Asclepias*)

Queen (*Danaus gilippus*)

Distinctive Marks Dark orange with black border. White dots on forewing. Wingspan 3 to 3½ inches.

Caterpillar Resembles Monarch but has wider black stripes, yellow spots, and three pairs of fleshy filaments. To 2½ inches long.

Range South

Habitat Open areas, gardens

Caterpillar Host Plants Milkweeds (*Asclepias*)

Skippers
FAMILY HESPERIIDAE

Named for their quick, darting flight, skippers resemble moths with their stout, hairy bodies and rather small wings held close to the body. They have wingspans of 1 to 2 inches, except giant skippers, which are to 3 inches. Like other butterflies they have knobbed antennae, but theirs end in hooks. Mostly small, in shades of brown and burnt orange, skippers can be a challenge to identify. There are more than 250 species in North America.

The caterpillars are smooth and dull in color, with a "neck" that enables them to bend backward and make leaf shelters for safety. (Small caterpillars cut a flap at the leaf edge, bend it back on the leaf top, and fasten it with a strand of silk. Larger ones fasten two leaves together with silk.) Pupating caterpillars may form loose cocoons in grass or leaf litter.

Folded-wing, or grass, skippers hold their wings at an angle, and look somewhat like folded paper airplanes while resting. Their caterpillars feed on grasses. Spread-wing skippers, which rest with wings open, favor other host plants such as legumes and mallows (*Malva, Sidalcea*). There are 13 species of giant skippers, such as the Yucca Skipper, mostly in the Southwest. They favor *Yucca* and *Agave* as host plants.

GRASS SKIPPERS

Fiery Skipper (*Hylephila phyleus*)

Distinctive Marks Orange with brown blotches; very short antennae. Wingspan 1 to 1¼ inches.

Caterpillar Variable: green, brown, or gray; brown vertical stripes; black head with dark marking behind head. To ¾ inch long.

Range East, Southwest

Habitat Lawns, fields

Caterpillar Host Plants Grasses (*Poa, Cynodon*)

Woodland Skipper (*Ochlodes sylvanoides*)

Distinctive Marks Burnt orange with brown blotches. Wingspan ¾ to 1⅛ inches.

Caterpillar Light green with dark vertical stripes; black head. To ¾ inch long.

Range Widespread in West

Habitat Extremely adaptable

Caterpillar Host Plants Grasses (*Phalaris, Cynodon*)

SPREAD-WING SKIPPERS

Common Checkered-Skipper (*Pyrgus communis*)

Distinctive Marks White checks on dark wings. Wingspan ¾ to 1¼ inches.

Caterpillar Tan with brown and white stripes on sides; black head. To ¾ inch long.

Range Widespread, except Northwest

Fiery Skipper

Habitat Disturbed areas

Caterpillar Host Plants Mallows (*Malva, Sidalcea*)

Silver-Spotted Skipper
(*Epargyreus clarus*)

Distinctive Marks Brown with diagonal orange band on forewing. Silver spot on underside of hindwing. Wingspan 2 to 2½ inches.

Caterpillar Yellow and green with large black head and narrow "neck." To 2 inches long.

Range Widespread, except in arid West

Habitat Open areas, gardens

Caterpillar Host Plants Wisteria, locust (*Robinia*)

Butterfly Biology

Eric Eaton

We tend to regard butterflies as diminutive birds, but, alas, they are mere insects. That beautiful Black Swallowtail lilting over the flowers was once a lowly larva, grazing on the dill or fennel in your garden. But whether we take note or not, butterflies are fascinating creatures at every stage of their lives, contributing much more than sheer beauty to natural ecosystems. While feeding on nectar, adult butterflies inadvertently pollinate many plants and allow them to reproduce. Eggs, caterpillars, and adult butterflies are important food sources for other organisms in the food web, such as birds, wasps, spiders, and small mammals. In the grand scheme of things, butterflies are indispensable, and a small fraction of the action is played out right in your own garden.

A Butterfly's Body

Far from being fragile, a butterfly is remarkably durable, its three-part body protected by an exoskeleton. The head is the sensory center, equipped with two antennae, two compound eyes, and a long proboscis, which uncoils to probe flowers for nectar. The thorax is the locomotion center; all six legs and four wings are attached to it. The abdomen is the reproductive and metabolic center that houses the sex organs and the digestive and excretory systems. Butterflies breath through tiny holes, called spiracles, along each side of the thorax and abdomen.

Millions of tiny scales coat the wings like shingles, giving butterflies their colorful appearance. Earth tones, such as brown, orange, yellow, white, and black, result from

Zebra Heliconians mating. In successful pairings, butterflies couple tail to tail. They can remain together for hours and sometimes fly off together.

pigment in the scales. The striking iridescent shades of blue, green, copper, and silver are given off by special scales that reflect light like a prism. This is why butterflies like blues or coppers often seem to change color right before your eyes. The scales are loosely attached, giving the wings a slippery quality and leaving a powdery residue on one's fingers after touching the insect. Nothing sticks to butterfly wings; this allows them to stay clean and occasionally lets butterflies escape spider webs.

How Butterflies Perceive the World

Butterflies literally look at things differently than we do. Actually, they rely less on sight and more on chemo-tactile senses to assess their surroundings. Female butterflies find the right plants for egg-laying by scratching the surface of foliage with their feet (tarsi) and "tasting" it to make sure that their caterpillars hatch on or near their required food plants. Butterfly antennae pick up and analyze airborne molecules, helping the insect to find flower nectar or a mate. Compound eyes create an enormous field of vision and sense motion far better than the human eye. Big eyes are all the better for detecting potential predators in all directions. They also help males to identify territorial competitors and the opposite sex. Butterfly eyes cannot resolve images very clearly, but they can see in the ultraviolet portion of the light spectrum.

Flowers often contain ultraviolet nectar guides on their petals, invisible to our eyes, that point pollinating insects toward their nectaries.

Butterfly Behavior

In the course of their lives, butterflies exhibit a wide array of behaviors. Males may establish territories and defend them against all intruders. Hackberry butterflies fly boldly at people, often alighting on them before returning to a perch nearby. Encounters between male sulphurs and whites may take the form of vertical "dogfights" that seem to spiral into the stratosphere before one party peels off. A male may hover over a perched female, wafting a seductive scent from special patches on his wings. In successful pairings, butterflies couple tail to tail, and sometimes they fly off together, one gender flapping with its passive partner in tow. They can remain together for hours.

Butterflies, which are ectothermic and depend on the ambient air temperature, often warm themselves by basking in a sunny spot in the morning hours. Some spread their wings flat, while others keep their wings closed and tilt them at an angle toward the sun's warming rays.

Not all butterflies seek nectar from flower blossoms. Some butterflies, such as anglewings and tortoiseshells, are more interested in fermenting tree sap, rotting fruit, animal droppings, carrion, even human sweat. In these species the adults hibernate and need extra nourishment in the form of amino acids and minerals that they get from these

A West Coast Lady derives nutrients from the salt in human sweat.

food sources to help them survive the winter, which they spend hidden under tree bark, in brush piles, or other sheltered spots. Male swallowtails, blues, and sulphurs congregate at the edges of puddles, taking in minerals and salts. They pass the nutrients on to females in sperm packets that enrich the eggs.

Survival Strategies

In all their life stages butterflies contend with a host of hazards: Predators, parasites, diseases, genetic defects, and chemicals decimate their numbers. Their best defense is an incredible capacity for reproduction. Females may lay many eggs, guaranteeing

The Miracle of Metamorphosis

Every butterfly goes through four different life stages. It begins life as an egg that's tinier than a pinhead in many cases. After approximately one week, the caterpillar, or larva, emerges, eats the eggshell as its first meal, and goes on an eating binge. The insect's mission is to accumulate enough fat reserves to get itself through the next step in its development, the pupal stage. The soft-bodied caterpillar has an exoskeleton, and inside every little caterpillar is a bigger one struggling to get out! During the growth process, which takes from two to four weeks in most cases, the caterpillar

The life cycle of a butterfly, the Gulf Fritillary: After it hatches from its egg, the caterpillar begins an eating binge. It grows and sheds its too-tight skin several times until it's ready to pupate.

develops embryonic wing buds and other adult features, all regulated by complex hormonal chemistry, and it molts its too-tight "skin" four or five times. (The interval between molts is called an "instar." The first instar begins at emergence from the egg, the second instar follows the first molt, and so on.) After shrugging off the old skin, the caterpillar inflates its body with air before the new skin can harden. At the end of several molts, the caterpillar has bulked up more than a thousandfold, stops eating, wanders restlessly in search of a place to pupate, and spins a little silken pad with its lower lip. From this pad it suspends itself upside-down (or horizontally, secured with a strand of silk) and molts one final time into a pupa, or chrysalis.

Despite its lifeless appearance, a chrysalis is, of course, a living organism, and during the pupal stage an enormous amount of energy is spent to rearrange the cellular structure of the caterpillar into that of a butterfly. From the outside the chrysalis may already resemble the adult butterfly, with clearly defined wing shapes, but inside a virtual cellular meltdown occurs.

After one to two weeks the new butterfly emerges wet and compact from its pupal case and slowly pumps fluid to inflate its crumpled wings. Some butterflies die during this laborious process or fail to unfurl their wings completely. During the hour or so that the insect is emerging and hardening its wings, it is extremely vulnerable to predators. Practically from the time its wings have hardened, the adult butterfly searches for a mate, so that the whole cycle can begin all over.

During the pupal stage, the cellular structure of the insect is arranged into that of an adult butterfly, which hatches after one to several weeks, or after overwintering, and starts looking for a mate.

Under ideal conditions, it takes one to two months from the time a female lays an egg until an adult butterfly emerges. But depending on latitude and species, there are many variables. In the South, there may be five or more generations in a year since butterflies can breed year-round. Tiger Swallowtails, for example, have up to three generations per year in southern areas and only one in northern climates. Monarchs have one very long-lived generation in late fall that migrates south, then another four or so while they are moving north from early spring to late summer.

In cold climates, admirals overwinter as tiny larvae inside leaves, then grow very quickly when spring brings new leaf growth on their host plants. Anglewings overwinter as adults, mate and lay eggs in early spring, and the larvae hatch in April or so. Other butterflies overwinter as chrysalides and don't emerge until late spring to mate; their larvae hatch in early summer.

that at least a fraction will reach maturity. The majority falls prey to nuthatches, creepers, and other birds, and to tiny wasps that lay their own eggs inside the butterfly's eggs.

Caterpillars are vulnerable to birds, parasitic wasps, spiders, and other animals, as well as to herbicides and pesticides. To avoid the majority of their enemies, many caterpillars feed at night. Some disguise their feeding patterns to leave less evidence, as birds know that damaged leaves are a clue to the presence of caterpillars. Many caterpillars are camouflaged by color and shape. A few, such as the Giant Swallowtail during its early stages of development, resemble bird droppings. Some swallowtail caterpillars sport false eyespots and, if threatened, stick out a forked gland (osmeterium) that smells bad and gives the caterpillar the appearance of a fork-tongued snake. Other caterpillars are brightly colored,

Some caterpillars, such as those of the Spicebush Swallowtail above, sport fake eyespots to confuse predators.

advertising their distasteful or toxic nature. The bold black, white, and yellow stripes of Monarch caterpillars are an example of warning colors. The larvae of many brush-footed butterflies, such as anglewings, Painted Ladies, and fritillaries are protected by a dense covering of branched spines. These wicked barbs make it difficult for birds to eat the larvae and for parasitic wasps to lay eggs on their soft bodies.

Stationary pupae may resemble a thorn or leaf, to evade parasitic wasps, birds, and other predators.

Adult butterflies may be pursued by birds or dragonflies, or ambushed at flowers by crab spiders and assassin bugs; others are hit by cars. Still, they are amazingly evasive, and tails and eyespots on the wings distract birds from the butterfly's more vulnerable body. If you have seen a swallowtail with a triangular bite where a tail should be, you know that tattered wings barely slow butterflies down. Some "tasty" butterflies also mimic poisonous butterflies in color and pattern. For example, the toxic Pipevine Swallowtail is mimicked by the Spicebush Swallowtail and the Red-Spotted Purple.

Butterfly Migration

Pat and Clay Sutton

While walking the beachfront one morning at Cape May Point, New Jersey, we noticed a few Red Admirals and a Question Mark flitting by. Then another Red Admiral zipped by, followed by others. Scanning down the beach and out over the Atlantic Ocean and Delaware Bay, we saw dozens of butterflies streaming in off the water. By noon, as the southerly breezes built, there were hundreds and hundreds passing, and as we did a 360-degree binocular scan, we saw nearly a hundred butterflies a minute, all surging north. This unusually huge migration on May 22, 2001, went on until dark, with legions of leps washing over the New Jersey shoreline.

Migration is defined as any seasonal movement between two areas. It is found throughout the animal kingdom and is quite common among insects such as butterflies and dragonflies. Many species of butterflies are highly migratory. Due to the butterflies' inability to fight strong winds, their migrations are usually not as concentrated as those of birds, but on rare occasions an amazing spectacle every bit as dramatic as the annual migrations of birds can be observed.

However, not all butterflies migrate; many are sedentary creatures. While afield you may see a Tiger Swallowtail disappear down a forest road, but it will probably not travel far beyond the neighborhood, town, or nearby forest. Some species of butterflies do not even wander. Generation after generation of Bog Coppers may be found only in and around a small bog where cranberry (*Vaccinium macrocarpon*), their only caterpillar food plant, grows. To find out how these and other species survive the colder months, see "Helping Butterflies Through the Winter," page 46.

Other butterflies, though, are short-, medium-, or even long-distance migrants, and these include some well-known favorites, such as Mourning Cloak, Painted Lady, American Lady, Red Admiral, and Common Buckeye. Over most of the country, some Mourning Cloaks, tortoiseshells, Question Marks, and various commas overwinter as adults, but local populations are almost always supplemented by fresh arrivals from the south each spring. American Ladies, Painted Ladies, Red Admirals, Common Buckeyes, and Variegated Fritillaries are cold-sensitive and cannot normally winter in northern areas due to the extreme winter temperatures. All arrive fresh in spring, migrating in from the south.

In fall, as temperatures drop and daylight hours shorten, descendants of these butterflies begin their migration south. Along the East Coast, steady streams of Mourning Cloaks, American Ladies, Painted Ladies, Red Admirals, and Common Buckeyes are seen heading south along with Monarchs, usually on gentle north or northwest tailwinds following a September or October cold front. Some of these cold-sensitive butterflies winter in the Southeast and Gulf states. Others, like the Painted Lady, are going to the southwestern states, northern Mexico, or even farther. Their offspring will then repopulate all the way north into Canada the following year.

Migrating Monarchs

The Monarch is the long-distance champion of butterfly migration, performing the longest migration of any insect in the world that we know. Each fall many millions of Monarchs, sometimes 250 million or more, empty out of the United States and southern Canada, east of the Rocky Mountains, and journey south to overwintering roosts in the mountain fir forests west of Mexico City. Monarchs from the northern edge of their summer range in Canada may migrate 3,000 miles to reach these winter roosts.

Monarchs are strong fliers, flying up to 20 miles an hour and sometimes at heights of over 10,000 feet. Monarch tagging has proved that they can travel at least 80 miles in a day. In the East, amazing concentrations of migrating Monarchs can be witnessed in September and October. Sometimes thousands of Monarchs can be seen roosting in eastern red cedars or clinging to stands of nectar-rich seaside goldenrod (*Solidago sempervirens*), which grows wild on coastal dunes. At this time blooming patches of Mexican sunflower (*Tithonia rotundifolia*), sedum, and New England aster (*Aster novae-angliae*) in backyard gardens might also be covered with migrant

Monarchs roosting for the night on an eastern red cedar, *Juniperus virginiana*, in Cape May, New Jersey, during their fall migration to their Mexican overwintering grounds.

Monarchs. Numbers can be almost unbelievable. In 1999, the Cape May Bird Observatory's Waterbird Migration Count at Avalon, New Jersey, on the Atlantic coast 16 miles north of Cape May, counted 85,659 Monarchs migrating by between September 22 and November 21, over half of them on one day in early October.

An often-asked question is, "Why aren't similar Monarch migrations seen in spring?" In spring, the migration is protracted, and it takes successive generations to repopulate the United States and Canada. Many short-lived generations move north in an incremental manner, laying eggs and dying, with their offspring moving farther north and eventually repopulating the summer range. In fall, individual Monarchs make the entire journey south and then overwinter.

A far smaller population of Monarchs (about 5 million) migrates from western states and British Columbia to overwintering sites along the California coast. There they congregate in groves of eucalyptus and Monterey pine (*Pinus radiata*) from just north of San Francisco to just south of Los Angeles. Recent research shows that some western Monarchs cross the Rocky Mountains and go to the Mexican winter roost sites.

Emigrating Butterflies

While a number of butterfly species migrate "both ways," north in the spring and

Help to Preserve an Endangered Phenomenon

The widely loved Monarch is not an endangered species; it has been known to rebound quickly after years of drought or snowstorms in its Mexican overwintering grounds. The continuation of its yearly migration from Canada to Mexico is far more uncertain. Scientists are so concerned about the future of Monarch migration that they have dubbed it an "endangered phenomenon." Deforestation in central Mexico degrades Monarch overwintering sites by opening up the forest canopy and creating an unfavorable microclimate for the clustering butterflies. Across the border on the U.S. side, milkweed is often targeted as a weed in agricultural areas, which means the critical food source for Monarch caterpillars is in jeopardy along the entire migration route.

While it is vitally important to support conservation efforts in Mexico, gardeners along the migration route can help Monarchs by growing milkweeds. The plants are sought for egg laying by northbound females in spring and by ensuing generations of Monarchs through the summer, while milkweed nectar attracts many species of butterflies, including Monarchs.

Nectar-rich fall-blooming flowers, such as goldenrod, *Solidago,* provide migrating Monarchs with much-needed nutrients to sustain them during their long journey to Mexico.

As the last generation of Monarchs for the year makes its arduous journey south in the fall, individuals can cover long distances in a day. They need an energy boost from nectar-rich flowers that bloom late in the season, such as joe-pye weed (*Eupatorium*), asters, goldenrods (*Solidago*), and sedums. At night, they look for safe roosting spots in the branches of trees and shrubs. Join with your neighbors to create safe-travel wildlife corridors of pesticide-free milkweeds, nectar plants, hedgerows, and trees.

Finally, support the efforts of Monarch Watch, Journey North, and other organizations, to fund research, preservation, tagging, and educational outreach (see "Organizations and Nurseries," page 112).

Claire Hagen Dole

south in the fall, the movement of many butterflies is one way only. In summer (particularly in late summer) and fall, many southern butterflies perform an irregular one-way emigration north, leaving their natal area and ending up far to the north of their normal range. This is an exciting time for butterfly watchers. In late summer and autumn butterfly watchers in Cape May eagerly await such southern species as the Cloudless Sulphur, Little Yellow, Sleepy Orange, Clouded Skipper, Fiery Skipper, Sachem, and even such rarities as the Gulf Fritillary, Long-Tailed Skipper, Eufala

A Painted Lady makes a pit stop during migration and sips nectar from New England aster, *Aster novae-angliae,* in fall.

Skipper, and Ocola Skipper. These are all species whose normal range is across the southern United States and further south into Mexico. In the West, California Tortoiseshells and American Snouts are particularly well known for their massive irruptions, at times involving many millions of butterflies.

Little understood by scientists, butterfly emigrations usually follow a good breeding season in the south. Adult butterflies may be reacting to overpopulation and the resulting depletion of food sources, both in caterpillar food plants and nectar plants. Emigrants may raise one or more broods far to the north of their usual range, but there is no return south for these species, and all eventually die, doomed by falling temperatures and the onset of winter. Nevertheless, this is the vehicle by which species expand their range, and in this age of global warming, a number of emigrants, such as Sachem and Little Yellow, are continually pushing the limits, extending their ranges farther north.

Some northern species irrupt as well, and New York-area butterfly watchers sometimes see southward movements of Compton Tortoiseshell, Milbert's Tortoiseshell, and even rarities such as Gray Comma. Their behavior may be little understood, but

Late-Blooming Perennials That Provide Nectar for Migrating Butterflies

Asclepias curassavica Bloodflower

Aster species Aster

Coreopsis verticillata Threadleaf coreopsis

Echinacea purpurea Purple coneflower

Eupatorium purpureum Joe-pye weed

Helenium autumnale Sneezeweed

Helianthus angustifolius
  Swamp sunflower

Liatris ligulistylis Meadow blazingstar

Scabiosa columbaria Pincushion flower

Sedum species Stonecrop

Solidago species Goldenrod

strays or vagrants far from their normal range create some of the most exciting moments in butterfly watching. We remember one balmy fall day when a Gulf Fritillary, found in a nearby butterfly garden, literally emptied the Cape May Hawkwatch Platform as avid visitors stampeded to see one of the first Cape May records for this butterfly in many years.

Understanding the complexities of butterfly migration is a major aspect of butterfly watching, and attracting migrants is one of the greatest pleasures of butterfly gardening. They may be here today and gone tomorrow, but a healthy and diverse butterfly garden can be an important pit stop where migrating butterflies can refuel for their continuing journey. This is particularly true for Monarchs and other "two-way" migrants such as Red Admiral and Painted Lady, but important even for emigrants. One early autumn day, our garden's regular "local" butterfly residents shared the asters and coneflowers (*Echinacea*) with such visitors as Cloudless Sulphur, Fiery Skipper, Ocola Skipper, and, amazingly, a robust Brazilian Skipper! Such is the joy of butterfly watching and gardening. Plant it and the migrants will come!

Turning Your Yard Into a Butterfly Sanctuary

Phil Schappert

Butterflies and other insects have two things going for them that most other conservation targets don't: They are relatively short-lived, and they are quite small. As with most other insects, butterflies have short generation times, and many species have multiple generations in a year or a season. What we do to their habitat right now often has a direct impact on their lives. And while it is true that some insects have large home ranges and others travel long distances, many spend their entire lives in areas not much larger than most backyards. The implications for butterfly conservation are pretty simple: If you plan and implement a butterfly garden with these thoughts in mind, you can provide an oasis of habitat that can sustain the entire life history of some butterflies.

Favorite nectar plants in this flower border include purple coneflower, *Echinacea purpurea,* blazingstars, *Liatris,* and oxeye daisy, *Heliopsis helianthoides.*

A Great Spangled Fritillary sips nectar from wild bergamot, *Monarda fistulosa,* a prairie wildflower. Masses of blooms are more attractive to butterflies than a few widely scattered plants.

Even simple, small changes can have pretty large impacts on the lives of the butterflies that frequent your garden. Think of your butterfly garden as a miniature wildlife preserve—even better, think of it as one in a chain of similar backyard sanctuaries—and you'll be well on your way to helping butterfly and other insect populations to not only persist in largely urban environments but thrive.

Fulfilling the Needs of Butterflies

Look at your neighborhood from a butterfly's perspective: Consider how far butterflies have to fly to find all the resources they need to live. How far will they have to travel if they can't find all they need in your backyard garden? If your neighbors also garden for wildlife, then you are well on your way to establishing a small network of butterfly habitats that can complement each other. Adjacent gardens provide corridors along which butterflies can move. The shorter its flights, the more likely it is that a butterfly will succeed in getting what it needs without falling prey to predators.

The way to turn your butterfly garden into a backyard sanctuary is to provide the necessary resources for all of a butterfly's life stages. Here are a few tips to help you create a butterfly-friendly environment.

Choose caterpillar food plants as well as nectar plants. One of the most important considerations is to make sure that in addition to nectar-rich flowers you include caterpillar host plants to give female butterflies places to lay their eggs and provide food for their caterpillars. Host plants don't only help keep female butterflies around your garden; they also help attract males looking for females.

It is unfortunate that many gardeners consider caterpillars pests, but I think—though I might be considered biased—that caterpillars are the most interesting part of the butterfly's life cycle. Of course, many gardeners fail to realize that where there are host plants and caterpillars, you can be sure that chrysalides will be found nearby and that there will eventually be more butterflies.

Give preference to native plants and wildflowers. The local butterflies that you are trying to attract to your garden have a history with the local plants. Given a choice between unknown, foreign plant species and locally native species, the butterflies will most likely prefer natives. Native plants also give a sense of place to your yard and to the community, making Tucson reflect the nearby desert while draping Tampa in tropical foliage.

Arrange plants thoughtfully. Most butterfly habitats include several layers, with a variety of plants at differing heights. To emulate nature's multilayered approach you should include plants that bloom at different heights, as well as small flowering shrubs that offer twigs to perch on. Consider adding a few vines to your plant choices

---

Event Releases

Thinking of sending colorful butterflies skyward instead of throwing rice at the bride and groom? Please think again. The unregulated sale and shipment of live butterflies has prompted the North American Butterfly Association, the Lepidopterists' Society, and other groups to issue a public statement against the practice. The concerns include spread of disease and inappropriate genetic mixing of different populations. Further, many butterflies are released out of range or season, condemning them to a quick death; and the high price commanded for Monarchs makes them targets for poachers in their winter range. Finally, years of meticulous research are rendered meaningless by willy-nilly releases. We suggest using rose petals; ask for outdated roses from florists.

Claire Hagen Dole

In addition to caterpillar host plants and nectar-rich flowers, a diverse butterfly garden includes places where butterflies can seek shelter to escape strong winds and rain, as well as places where they can perch and warm their bodies, as the blues above.

since these often bloom at various heights. Masses of blooms, or the close proximity of caterpillar host plants, are more attractive to butterflies than widely spaced plants, so give some thought to mass plantings of particularly attractive species like Mexican sunflowers (*Tithonia*) or asters.

Pick plants for every season. Attract adult butterflies with colorful flowers that offer nectar from spring through fall, or choose a variety of plants that bloom at different times of the season to achieve the same effect. It is also useful to provide a range of suitable host plants for multi-brooded species. For example, provide Monarchs with early-blooming milkweeds that may die back halfway through summer as well as late-blooming species that provide suitable egg-laying sites later in the season.

Create a sunny corner. Butterflies need some open, sunny spaces, out of the wind, where they can bask. Their bodies depend on the temperature of the air around them, and they need sunshine to warm up to flight temperature. Consider not covering every square inch of your garden with plants but instead leaving a low, protected sunny corner or even a centrally located spot as a butterfly sunning area.

Provide shelter and perches. Butterflies also need sheltered areas to escape strong winds and rain. Unfortunately, so-called "butterfly houses" rarely achieve their goal (although they do make good refuges for predators like spiders and wasps, which help in the biological control of garden pests). Instead, a border of shrubs and trees can provide host plants for larvae, as well as dry places where butterflies can hide from bad weather or predators. Untended edges of grasses, clovers, and dandelions also provide shelter and early nectar for certain species. Some butterflies also require perches where they can watch for mates, so tall herbs or small flowering shrubs can serve a dual purpose.

Set up a spot for puddling. In addition to the nectar they sip from plants, most species need to acquire compounds that they cannot get from plants. Many of these are mineral salts that are naturally available in the soil of your garden. An empty sandy spot under a bird bath or dripper where the soil is often wet is the perfect spot for butterflies to gather on the ground and get the additional nutrients they need.

A wet sandy spot invites butterflies, such as these Spring Azures, to puddle. Butterflies acquire nutrients not available from plants by taking up mineral salts from the soil.

Relax your neat and tidy standards. A garden that looks and acts more like nature is not only easier on the person maintaining it but also allows habitat to develop for butterflies at all four life stages. Leave a corner of your yard untended, allowing native grasses to grow and feed larvae of skippers and satyrs. Don't remove clovers; they provide early nectar to a variety of insects and are larval host plants for sulphurs, blues, and skippers. In autumn, let fallen leaves create a natural mulch—where moths and skippers pupate—before the leaf litter decomposes into nutrients for your garden.

Lose the lawn. Plan to reduce or eliminate lawn, which offers nothing to wildlife, wastes precious water, and is a major source of pesticide and herbicide contamination of our waterways and lakes.

Hold the poisons. One caveat that should be readily appreciated by anyone with a butterfly garden is that the use of pesticides—even so-called biological control agents such as Bt (*Bacillus thuringiensis*), which kills all caterpillars indiscriminately—should be strictly controlled or, even better, avoided altogether (see box on page 43). Stick

Butterfly conservation in action: Creating public butterfly sanctuaries as well as backyard butterfly gardens provides much-needed habitat for butterflies and other wildlife.

with natural products such as insecticidal soaps or plant-derived oils for those rare occasions when pest control is needed. I rarely use even natural pesticides in my garden, preferring to let nature take its own course—which, in my case, includes letting lizards, spiders, wasps, ants, and other insect predators do the dirty work for me. My way of thinking is, why should I pay for what nature will do free of charge?

Looking Beyond Your Butterfly Sanctuary

If butterflies are worth attracting to your garden, aren't they also worth having in local parks, public gardens, and natural areas? And to ensure that there are butterflies available to come to your garden, don't you also need to help protect them everywhere?

My best advice is to be proactive rather than reactive. Don't wait for butterflies to become endangered, but work now to help keep them safe. For example, ask local or state agencies to cease, or at least limit, roadside pesticide spraying; ask them to ensure that roadside mowing is rotated through the seasons instead of always being done at the same time in the same place each year; and to use native plants wherever possible. Any of these initiatives that you can conduct on a wide scale will help you have butterflies always—the flying flowers of the insect world—in your own backyard sanctuary to watch and enjoy.

Inviting Caterpillars Into Your Garden

Claire Hagen Dole

Early naturalists believed that caterpillars and butterflies were separate, unrelated insects. How surprised they would have been by the notion of gardening to attract caterpillars! Yet, to further the cause of butterflies, providing host plants that feed the caterpillars is as important as filling flower beds with bright, nectar-rich blooms that provide nourishment for the adults.

If they find the plants they need for their offspring in your garden, female butterflies may lay eggs there, creating a new generation that grows to maturity in your yard. It's an effective way to boost local butterfly populations, and the four-part life cycle (see box on pages 26–27) is fascinating to watch.

Finding the Right Caterpillar Host Plants

How do you decide what plants would be best? Browse through the illustrations in "Butterfly Families," page 4, and try to identify the wandering butterflies brought into your garden by nectar-rich flowers. Also check a butterfly guide to find other species that may occur in your region and might be tempted to visit if they found the right host plants. Then pick out promising caterpillar plants to encourage the adult butterflies to linger. In general, think native plants when landscaping for caterpillars. Local butterflies and other insects have evolved with native plants and are adapted to them. For specific recommendations of caterpillar host plants, see "Encyclopedia of Butterfly and Caterpillar Plants," page 67.

If you provide the host plants they need for their offspring in your yard, female butterflies may lay eggs there, creating a new generation that grows to maturity in your garden. Caterpillars, clockwise from top left: Brown Elfin, Pipevine Swallowtail, Checkered White, and Cloudless Sulphur.

Providing the right caterpillar host plants is crucial for success, as many caterpillars are picky eaters that require specific food plants. Milbert's Tortoiseshell caterpillars only accept nettles (*Urtica*). Monarch caterpillars primarily feed on milkweeds (*Asclepias*). As they fly north from Mexico in the spring, adult females look for milkweeds on which to lay their eggs. It's a great help to the butterflies if gardeners on the migration route provide these critical caterpillar host plants. Obviously, planting a few milkweeds doesn't offset the massive loss of habitat that progresses daily as a result of urban sprawl and changes in rural land use, but every step counts.

How do you know if caterpillars have made their home in your garden? Look for chewed leaves (a caterpillar may be on the leaf or nearby) or frass (dark pellets of excrement) on leaves or leaf axils. Some larvae feed communally; look for batches of Mourning Cloak larvae on willows. Other caterpillars may make a communal silk nest, such as Milbert's Tortoiseshells on nettles. Individual larvae, such as Painted Lady caterpillars, may rest in a silken "hammock" on a leaf, then emerge to feed at night. In winter, look for a rolled leaf that is still attached to an otherwise bare cherry (*Prunus*), willow (*Salix*), or poplar (*Populus*); inside may be a tiny admiral caterpillar.

Creating a Caterpillar-Friendly Environment

To emulate nature, locate favored host plants in different parts of the garden. In nature, caterpillars are usually scattered over an area, instead of clustering together on one bush. Spread out, they are less vulnerable to predators and other dangers. An adult female lays eggs singly or in clusters, on leaves or buds of host plants. It's vital to her offspring's survival that she choose well. She scratches the leaf surface with her feet, giving the plant a kind of chemical taste test for compatibility. She determines if the plant supplies enough tender new growth and visually checks the plant for other eggs or larvae to ensure that there will be enough greenery for the growing caterpillars. If there's too much activity already, she looks for an unoccupied plant.

American Lady caterpillar.

How you site caterpillar host plants in your garden depends largely on where you live and what butterflies you are trying to interest in your offerings. In general it's best to approximate the plants' native habitat. It's a good way to create an environment that is appealing to the female butterflies that search out the plants.

Providing leaf mulch or low-growing plants—instead of leaving the ground bare or spreading coarse bark—is important to protect caterpillars that hide out during the day and feed at night when they are better protected against predators. Fritillary caterpillars, for example, do not spend all of their time on the foliage of their host plant, violet (*Viola*), instead hiding in leaf litter or low vegetation during the daytime. The caterpillars of skippers need leaf mulch when they are ready to pupate.

Natural Pest Controls That Kill Caterpillars

Many people don't realize that *Bt* (*Bacillus thuringiensis*), promoted as a safe and natural insecticide, kills all moth and butterfly larvae—not just targeted species, such as the gypsy moth. Talk to your neighbors about creating a chemical-free landscape of diverse plantings, where wildlife can move in safely. Also bear in mind that parasitic wasps, being marketed to gardeners as controls for aphids, tomato hornworms, and European corn borers among others, are nonspecific and kill butterfly eggs and caterpillars as well. Praying mantises kill adult butterflies; ladybird beetles eat eggs.

Be mindful of caterpillars when you clean up the garden in fall, disturbing the ground as little as possible and leaving stalks of herbaceous perennials and grasses in place. Tiger swallowtails, for example, look for rough bark, fenceposts, or sturdy plant stalks when they are ready to pupate in fall. Skippers and moths pupate in ground litter and are very vulnerable to any kind of disturbance.

Silver-Spotted Skipper caterpillar.

Caterpillar Appetites

If you're a bit reluctant to invite hordes of munching arthropods to lunch, keep in mind that nature has a plan: Larvae are an important, protein-rich link in the food web. They attract many birds, lizards, and small mammals, as well as wasps and spiders, to your garden: Survival rate from butterfly egg to adult may be as low as one in a hundred; that's why female butterflies lay so many eggs. And should some caterpillars become too voracious, relocate some individuals to another plant of the same species. Most plants will survive moderately heavy defoliation; keeping caterpillars in check is more of an aesthetic consideration.

Also consider preferred caterpillar diets: In most cases, they won't be interested in prized ornamental shrubs or flowers. They would much rather eat "weedy" plants, such as clovers (*Trifolium*), nettles (*Urtica*) or plantains (*Plantago*), which are found in most yards.

And what about the so-called pests? The green-, yellow-, and black-striped larvae of the Black Swallowtail that you may see in your vegetable garden feeding on parsley (*Petroselinum crispum*), dill (*Anethum graveolens*), and carrot tops (*Daucus carota*) are often considered a nuisance. These caterpillars originally fed only on native plants such as angelica (*Angelica*), but they have also adapted to eat nonnative herbs in the parsley family, Apiaceae. So all a gardener needs to do is

Black Swallowtail caterpillar.

Rearing Butterfly Caterpillars

Sooner or later, you may want to try rearing caterpillars in a screened container, such as an inexpensive terrarium. This is a great project for kids, who will enjoy searching for larvae in the garden or along the roadside. Collect a half dozen or so caterpillars on a branch of their host plant. Keep the plant fresh in a container of water, with paper towels around the opening to keep caterpillars from falling in and drowning. If the host plant is not close at hand, pick enough to keep in a plastic bag in the refrigerator. Put in new foliage every couple of days, carefully transferring the caterpillars. Or leave for a few hours to allow the caterpillars to crawl onto new foliage. Keep paper towels on the floor of the container to catch frass (excrement), and change daily to keep the area clean and disease-free. Situate the container away from direct sunlight.

A caterpillar goes through four instars, or developmental stages, before molting its skin one final time and becoming a chrysalis. Provide a stout branch on which the larva can attach itself when ready to pupate. In order to emerge properly, the adult butterfly needs to push against something. Some caterpillars pupate against the screen on top, hanging like ornaments until ready to emerge. Fall-pupating butterflies, such as Tiger Swallowtails, will spend the winter as chrysalides. Make sure they are kept in a cool place, such as an unheated garage, so they don't miscalculate and emerge during the winter months. Mist periodically to prevent desiccation.

scatter a few extra patches of parsley and dill throughout the garden to disperse the caterpillars and allow for their huge appetites.

The Gray Hairstreak chooses a lot of host plants, one of which is green bean. Larvae may work their way through one large bean, but are not likely to consume your whole bean crop. The beautiful Long-Tailed Skipper uses green beans as well; its larva, the bean leaf roller, feeds on the leaves, but it is not voracious. Try to identify larvae and destroy only the offspring of destructive pests, such as gypsy moths, cutworms, and tent caterpillars.

The familiar Cabbage White, which feeds on plants in the mustard family (Brassicaceae), often gets unfairly blamed for damage by the Cabbage Looper moth. You can lure the Cabbage White away from your arugula with nasturtium (*Tropaeolum majus*); its leaves contain oils that are chemically similar.

One small yard may not seem too promising as caterpillar habitat, but don't forget that there may be environments nearby that feed and shelter caterpillars as well.

Helping Butterflies Through the Winter

Bernard S. Jackson

Have you ever wondered where butterflies go at night, or when it rains? They may seek shelter in the cavity of a tree trunk or under the leaves of a dense shrub. Many butterflies crawl down grass stems to hide in denser vegetation when a storm threatens or night falls.

Waiting out the long, cold winter months is a different story. Monarchs migrate to communal roosting sites in Mexico and along the California coast in fall, preferring to spend the winter in a cool, moist climate. Other butterflies have evolved a number of strategies to survive the rigors of northern winters. In autumn, the Bog Copper lays eggs on its host plant, wild cranberry (*Vaccinium macrocarpon*), ensuring that a new generation will carry on in spring. The Red-Spotted Admiral overwinters as a tiny caterpillar inside a rolled leaf, fastened

The Red-Spotted Admiral overwinters as a tiny caterpillar inside a rolled-up leaf fastened to a tree branch with silk.

with silk to a branch of willow (*Salix*) or black cherry (*Prunus serotina*).

Many butterflies overwinter in the chrysalis stage. In fall, swallowtail caterpillars seek out secluded resting places—a branch or the underside of a windowsill—where they can pupate. Others, such as the Spring Azure, may drop to the ground and pupate inside a dead, curled-up leaf or beneath accumulating leaf litter.

A few species hibernate as adults. Anglewings and tortoiseshells stay in their summer range and hibernate individually and may awaken briefly on a sunny winter day. Some, including the Green Comma and the Mourning Cloak, sit tight through the cold weather as far north as Alaska.

To survive winter, chrysalides and adult butterflies must be protected from rain or snow, chilling winds, intense light, and predators. They usually overwinter tucked into such places as old woodpecker holes, behind exfoliating bark, among the nooks and crannies of wood or rock piles and dry-stone walls, among leaf piles, in fallen hollow logs, even behind the clapboarding of a house or shed.

When I was a boy in England, before the days of central heating, Small Tortoiseshell and Peacock butterflies used to overwinter inside the house behind wardrobes, picture frames, or curtains. When the spring sun warmed the house again, they would stir themselves, and we would fling wide the windows lest they beat themselves against the glass.

Winter Homes for Butterflies

Those of us who like to see butterflies around our gardens may wonder how we can give these lovely creatures a helping hand during winter. It bears repeating that an informal, natural garden is more welcoming to wildlife than a neatly trimmed property, no matter what the season. If seedpods and stalks of herbaceous perennials are left in place in fall as well as leaf litter, insects can find shelter for the winter and birds

The Mourning Cloak overwinters as an adult, seeking shelter in a pile of dead leaves, for example.

can forage. Provided that grassy areas and host plants are left alone in fall, gardeners needn't worry too much about butterflies that overwinter in the egg stage.

Small Hibernation Shelters: Gardeners can do a few things for butterflies that overwinter in one of the other life stages. Adult Mourning Cloak butterflies, for example, may lie flat on the ground, under pieces of board, or even inside discarded tin cans. They may also crawl into piles of dead leaves caught up in some dry out-of-the-way corner. They may readily seek out supplemental hibernation shelters provided by gardeners. A large juice can or open-ended wooden box works well. Stuff it lightly with dry leaves (oak leaves or others that retain their stiffness are best), and place it in an area frequented by butterflies, perhaps by an evergreen tree next to a flower bed or against the base of the garden shed. Be sure to position the can or box in a sheltered spot above ground, to avoid close proximity to predators, such as shrews. Raise the back of the shelter slightly so that water does not run in. Voilà—a cozy retreat, where adult anglewings and tortoiseshells can while away the winter months.

Another option is to invert a can over the top of a round post to provide shelter. Choose a can that fits loosely over the post to allow the butterflies enough room to creep in and upward. A single nail driven through the end of the can well into the post will hold it steady. A rubber gasket will prevent water from seeping in around the nail hole.

Let a climbing vine clamber up the post: It will camouflage the tin and provide food and shelter for many types of wildlife. Consider North American native plants, such as coral honeysuckle (*Lonicera sempervirens*) or climbing aster (*Aster carolinianus*), both host plants for checkerspots. American wisteria (*Wisteria frutescens*), a host plant for skippers, is a strong climber useful on taller structures. Avoid English ivy (*Hedera helix*), a popular evergreen climber that offers little to wildlife and is considered an invasive pest in coastal areas. (For more information, visit the web site of the Southeast Exotic Pest Plant Council, www.se-eppc.org.)

It can be surprising to see just how small a crevice butterflies can crawl into. They don't necessarily have to walk upright into a shelter, but can sidle in flat on their sides. Entrances and interiors of wintering sites therefore need not be all that spacious. Butterflies often wedge themselves under loose tree bark; try nailing a piece of bark loosely against a fencepost to provide shelter for local brushfoot butterflies that over-winter as adults, as well as edge-of-the-wood butterflies, such as Green Commas, Mourning Cloaks, and Tiger Swallowtails that need safe places for their chrysalides.

I have often witnessed overwintering Milbert's Tortoiseshells emerging from dry stone walls around farm fields and woodland edges. As these walls are built without the use of mortar, they offer numerous nooks and crannies for adult butterflies to creep into or for caterpillars to pupate in. A dry-stone wall, especially one that's next to a flower bed, adds greatly to the general appearance and value of a wildlife garden.

Piles of sticks, brush, poles, or old lumber stacked upright against the garden shed or around the trunk of a dead tree will also offer shelter to butterflies, as will a free-standing "wigwam" of the same materials.

Large-Scale Hibernation Shelters: My favorite wintering site is a log pile especially built for butterflies and not managed as a source of firewood. Several years ago, I constructed a number of log piles for the Memorial University Botanical Garden in St. John's, Newfoundland, where winters are harsh indeed. I used salvaged logs with the bark still attached, each measuring four to six feet in length and at least two inches in diameter. I laid a first layer of logs on the ground, spacing the logs from four inches to a foot apart, and the second layer perpendicular to the first, creating a series of squares and open spaces. Before adding the final layer of logs, I placed a layer of roof-ing felt to make the pile waterproof. The resulting structures were fairly large—about six feet by five feet, and four feet high—and may be more suitable for use on a large piece of land, but they can easily be scaled down in size for home gardens.

Top: Short-Tailed Swallowtails on a log. Inset: A log pile provides shelter for butterflies and other small creatures.

A vine that grows up and over it softens the look of the pile. I used hops (*Humulus lupulus*), an attractive vine that hosts larvae of the Eastern Comma and Red Admiral. Virginia creeper (*Parthenocissus quinquefolia*) will eagerly sprawl or climb. Its berries are sought out by downy woodpeckers, and its leaves feed the larvae of the Eight-Spotted Forester and Lettered Sphinx moths. In fall, the leaves turn brilliant red.

A whole ecosystem will develop inside the log pile during winter: Predators like snakes, spiders, and beetles share space with decomposers such as millipedes, sowbugs, fungi, and bacteria. Mice stash seeds and raise their young, while birds seek an insect meal. The pile may even attract bats.

As with other homemade wintering sites, log piles should be constructed where adult butterflies or pupating larvae can conveniently find them. If possible, find a sheltered location close to an abundance of fall-blooming nectar plants, such as asters, goldenrod (*Solidago*), and meadow blazingstar (*Liatris ligulistylis*).

Of course, the key to attracting the butterflies that need good winter homes, such as anglewings and tortoiseshells, is to install the caterpillar host plants they require: nettles (*Urtica*), willows (*Salix*), hops (*Humulus*), and hackberries (*Celtis*). Once you find caterpillars feeding on these plants, you are well on your way to establishing resident populations. In autumn, the adults will be looking for shelter from winter's storms.

Butterfly Meadows

Claire Hagen Dole

Picture a sunny wildflower meadow, humming with the activity of bees, dragonflies, and colorful butterflies. Sparrows feed on seeds of Indian grass as it sways in the breeze. Closer to the ground, caterpillars munch on grass blades, waiting to turn into tawny skippers at summer's end.

It's a powerful image, reminding us of carefree childhood days. Little wonder that wildflower seed mixes, packaged in attractive packets and cans, are a booming business. Offering an inexpensive assortment of flowers and the promise of an easy-care landscape that does double duty as prime wildlife habitat, these mixes can be irresistible.

Establishing a successful wildflower meadow, however, is not quite as easy as shaking seeds from a can. It's important to select the right mix for your area and to invest time and effort in proper site preparation and maintenance.

Meadows in the Wild

In nature, meadows or prairies, terms used to describe North American grasslands, can grow in dry, medium, or moist soils. Composed primarily of regionally different grasses and punctuated by the colorful blossoms of wildflowers, meadows are transitory places. In many places, trees will eventually sprout, and the meadows become part of the forests that edge them. In areas where the soil is dry, meadows are more resistant to encroaching trees: Periodic burning keeps larger woody plants in check, breaks grass-seed dormancy and, to a lesser degree, helps to recycle nutrients and enrich the soil.

In a meadow, many bunch grasses thrive, such as Indian grass (*Sorghastrum nutans*), broom sedge (*Andropogon virginicus*), and prairie dropseed (*Sporobolus heterolepsis*). They form separate clumps rather than spread by underground roots, and leave growing spaces for wildflowers, which they help prop up. Bunch grasses also feed and shelter birds, insects, and small mammals. They are caterpillar host plants for skippers and satyrs.

Legumes, such as purple prairie clover (*Dalea purpurea*), lupines (*Lupinus*), vetches (*Vicia*), and false indigos (*Baptisia*), make up a large and important family of North American meadow wildflowers. Legumes fix nitrogen in the soil and are caterpillar hosts for sulphurs, hairstreaks, blues, and skippers.

A midwestern meadow features oxeye daisy, *Heliopsis helianthoides,* and wild bergamot, *Monarda fistulosa.*

Meadow Mixes for Every Purpose

While there are many cover-the-country wildflower mixes on the market, seed companies also create specialized blends that are meant for attracting butterflies or hummingbirds, for xeriscaping, or for a specific geographic region. There is even a wildflower mat, with seeds imbedded into biodegradable fiber.

All-purpose butterfly seed mixes aren't very different from generic meadow mixes. They tend to rely heavily on annual wildflowers, such as California poppy (*Eschscholzia californica*) and cornflower, or bachelor's button (*Centaurea cyanus*), a European invasive that's a serious pest in native grasslands and agricultural areas. Annuals such as these are added to make a colorful splash the first year, while perennials are getting established. The perennials in the mixes are often weedy exotics that are guaranteed to grow

Lupines, *Lupinus,* and other wildflowers and grasses in a Rocky Mountain meadow.

almost anywhere: Queen Anne's lace (*Daucus carota*), wallflowers (*Erysimum*), and dame's rocket (*Hesperis matronalis*), now considered a noxious weed in Colorado.

Regional mixes are a much better bet in terms of content as well as quality. It's best to choose a mix that was formulated to target your local ecosystem, for example, a Texas prairie mix or a West Coast mix. You can find mixes of native perennials and grasses at specialty nurseries and public utilities that promote water conservation. A well-chosen regional mix can make a fine butterfly meadow.

Creating your own meadow mix of nectar and caterpillar host plants is another easy option. Your local native plant society can provide you with plant lists and information on establishing wildflowers. Some nurseries will custom-blend seeds or sell individual packets of native wildflower seeds.

Wildflower Seed Mixes Under Scrutiny

Wildflower seed mixes didn't pass the test at the University of Washington. According to a study by Lorraine Brooks, of the UW Center for Urban Horticulture, when researchers grew seeds from 19 different packets of seed mix, they identified several invasive species in every mix and noxious weed seeds in 8 of the mixes. Seeds were often listed inaccurately or not at all. Their recommendation? Use individual packets of regionally native wildflowers.

Start a meadow from seed in fall or set out small plants in early summer, as shown here.

Planting a Meadow

Meadow gardening is a learning process; start small the first year and expand in future seasons. Before you open that seed packet, give your very best effort to clearing the site of weeds. For success, the site must be free of perennial weeds. Smother weeds with black plastic or newspapers during the hot summer months. In the fall, clean up the cooked vegetation and rake the soil lightly. Scatter grass seeds and wildflower seeds and cover with one-half inch of soil; tamp it down. The seeds will germinate in spring; in the meantime they benefit from winter's freezing and thawing. Confused about how to tell the desirable plants from the weeds? In spring, start a flat of wildflower mix indoors and compare the seedlings with those emerging outdoors.

If you don't want to wait a year for wildflowers, start separate plugs of grasses and wildflower mix indoors in early spring. Then go out and weed the site, water and weed again until the site is weed-free. In early summer, plant the grass plugs about a foot apart, and intersperse with wildflower plugs. Mulch to keep weeds down.

Many meadow gardeners have been defeated by weeds like Canada thistle (*Cirsium arvense*) and multiflora rose (*Rosa multiflora*). Be vigilant against the worst invaders, but consider leaving a few exotic plants that are useful to insects, such as plantains (*Plantago*) for Common Buckeye caterpillars and dock (*Rumex*) for the caterpillars of several coppers. If you're very lucky, long-dormant seeds of native plants may sprout; be sure to check a guidebook before removing any unfamiliar plants.

It's not unusual for native perennials to take up to three years to bloom. Once established, they will perform for years with little care. They will attract a host of native pollinators and birds, making your meadow a richly diverse habitat.

Managing the Meadow

Don't be a neatnik in late fall, when blossoms fade and the meadow takes on an unkempt appearance. Learn to love the subtle beauty of golden grass plumes and winter-brown seedpods, especially when covered with a rime of frost. Resident wildlife will thank you for leaving the meadow intact throughout the winter. Tiny larvae of blues

---

Great Butterfly Plants for the Meadow

PERENNIALS

Aster laevis (Symphiotrichum laevis) Smooth aster

Baptisia bracteata Cream false indigo

Coreopsis lanceolata Lance-leafed coreopsis

Echinacea purpurea Purple coneflower

Eriogonum umbellatum Sulphur flower

Gaillardia aristata Blanket flower

Liatris ligulistylis Meadow blazingstar

Lupinus perennis Wild lupine

Monarda citriodora Lemon mint

Dalea purpurea Purple prairie clover

Ratibida pinnata Gray-headed coneflower

Rudbeckia hirta Black-eyed susan

Solidago rigida Stiff goldenrod

Viola pedata Birdsfoot violet

GRASSES FOR ALL REGIONS

Bouteloua curtipendula Side-oats grama

Elymus canadensis Canada wild rye

Panicum virgatum Switchgrass

Schizachyrium scoparium Little bluestem

Sorghastrum nutans Indian grass

GRASSES FOR THE SOUTHEAST AND FLORIDA

Eragrostis spectabilis Purple love grass

Muhlenbergia capillaris Gulf muhly

GRASSES FOR THE SOUTHWEST

Muhlenbergia rigens Deer grass

Achnatherum hymenoides Indian rice grass

GRASSES FOR THE PACIFIC COAST

Festuca californica California fescue

Nassella lepida Foothill feather grass

Liatris ligulistylis, meadow blazingstar.

Once established, native wildflowers in your butterfly meadow, such as purple prairie clover, *Dalea purpurea,* purple coneflower, *Echinacea purpurea,* and butterfly weed, *Asclepias tuberosa,* will perform for years with little care. They will attract a host of native pollinators and birds, making your meadow a richly diverse habitat.

overwinter inside lupine seedpods, while satyr larvae attach themselves to grass blades. Birds will pick over seedheads and later glean fibers for nesting material. In spring, meadowlarks, field sparrows, and quail nest in the cover of grass clumps.

Mowing is probably the trickiest part of meadow management. No matter at what time of the year you mow, you will disturb wildlife. The best advice for overall wildlife management is to rotate sections, either year to year or within a year. For example, mow part of the meadow in late winter, and part in midsummer after birds have fledged. Cut half of the meadow to a height of about six inches. Let debris sit for a couple of days before removing, so insects and others can relocate. The following year or season, cut the other half, then rotate each year. Varying your mowing schedule will also prevent any given plant species from gaining overall dominance, thus maximizing the diversity of plant species in the meadow.

Herbs for Butterflies

Jim and Dotti Becker

Herbs are the plants that we use in our everyday lives. Pick up any book about herbs and you will find chapters extolling their virtues in cooking, teas, medicines, cosmetics, and dyes. If these aren't enough reasons to grow herbs, the descriptions of their wonderful scented foliage and flowers will certainly persuade anyone to add some to the garden. However, one of the greatest pleasures gained by growing herbs is not mentioned in most books: They are outstanding plants for attracting butterflies and other pollinating insects.

What could be more delightful than sitting on a sun-warmed bench and watching two swallowtails flutter skyward in a ritual dance, skippers darting from lavender to lavender, or a boldly striped Monarch caterpillar munching on butterfly weed? Herb gardening for butterflies is certainly "for use and for delight." All of the things that lure butterflies—nectar-bearing flowers, food for caterpillars, and sheltering trees or large shrubs—are easily found among the herbs. Thoughtfully arranged, these elements will keep butterflies in your garden throughout the growing season.

It's important to keep three essentials in mind when you place herbs in your garden: diversity, mass, and constancy. Be sure to include a variety of flower colors, corolla lengths, and flower shapes to attract a wide range of butterfly species. Use masses of flowers; single plants simply won't do. Finally, keep a constant supply of flowers throughout the seasons, from early spring to late autumn. You may be surprised to see some butterflies out in all but the coldest months of the year. In our

To attract butterflies, plant masses of different herbs to provide food and host plants for the entire growing season. Above, a Tiger Swallowtail sips nectar on lavender, a favorite herb.

Oregon garden the first butterfly sighting is usually an early-March Mourning Cloak, and there are often skippers on the wing late into October.

Favorite Butterfly Herbs

Butterflies are very particular about their flowers. You have surely noticed that some flowers are just aflutter with butterflies and bees, while others are snubbed completely.

One of our favorite butterfly herbs is lavender. In our garden, the English lavenders (*Lavandula angustifolia* cultivars) bloom from late June until mid-July, the lavandins (*Lavandula* × *intermedia* cultivars) from early July until mid-August, and spike lavender (*Lavandula latifolia*) from late August until nearly November. This mix provides flowers throughout the summer and autumn. All three types are very attractive to a wide range of butterflies, including Monarchs, whites, skippers, and swallowtails. Spike lavender is especially important because of its long blooming period. It is an autumn oasis for late-flying skippers, American Ladies, Common Buckeyes, and bumblebees. As other flowers fade, the concentration of insects converging on it reaches frantic proportions. This is also a preferred plant for other animals; dark-eyed juncos are fond of the seeds, which ripen in late autumn.

Two other midsummer bloomers that maintain a flurry of insects are oregano (*Origanum vulgare*) and woolly applemint (*Mentha × villosa*). Both of these herbs create awe-inspiring clumps of color and motion, and the pleasant humming of tiny wings. The oregano can either be the white-flowered and green-bracted culinary type (*Origanum vulgare* subsp. *hirtum*) or the purple-bracted species known as wild marjoram (*Origanum vulgare* subsp. *vulgare*). The latter is the preferred flower of the beautiful Ctenucha moth, whose larvae feed on grasses. This slow-fluttering daytime flier has a flaming body of orange and blue, and its charcoal-colored wings are adorned with delicate crescent moons on the undersides. The woolly applemint holds our garden record for hosting the largest number of insects and the greatest diversity of insect species. Often seen together are small butterflies like hairstreaks and skippers, bumblebees, honeybees, and Ctenucha moths, as well as thread-waisted and sand wasps.

A Gray Hairstreak on nectar-rich oregano, *Origanum vulgare*, an herb popular with many butterflies.

Some herbs, such as sages (*Salvia*), may generally be more attractive to hummingbirds, but there are also varieties that draw butterflies. For example, garden sage (*Salvia officinalis*) and the red-flowering pineapple sage (*Salvia elegans*) attract swallowtails and sulphurs.

A number of Native American herbs have showy flowers and are great nectar sources for butterflies. You may already have some of them in your garden, like butterfly weed (*Asclepias tuberosa*), purple coneflower (*Echinacea purpurea*), and bee balm (*Monarda didyma*). Look, too, for their less common relatives. Wild bergamot (*Monarda fistulosa*) and mint-leafed bergamot (*Monarda fistulosa* var. *menthifolia*) have more delicately colored flowers and some mildew resistance. Yellow coneflower (*Echinacea paradoxa*) and pale coneflower (*Echinacea pallida*) do well in dry sites. The mountain mints (*Pycnanthemum*), favored by many small butterfly species, and the joe-pye weeds

During inclement weather, butterflies may hide under the large leaves of elecampane, *Inula helenium*.

(*Eupatorium*), favorites of the Monarch, also deserve more recognition as attractive, easy-to-grow perennials. Don't forget to add some native goldenrods (*Solidago*). They add a splash of yellow to the waning autumn garden and are valuable for their late-season nectar.

Humble dandelion also deserves a mention here. Butterflies that spend the winter as adults, such as tortoiseshells, depend on this early-blooming herb for their first spring meal. You probably won't need to plant dandelions. Just be a bit happier when you see them pop up around your lawn and garden.

If you provide a steady supply of nectar-bearing flowers, the lingering butterflies may even mate in your garden. There are many herbs that are hosts for caterpillars: dill (*Anethum graveolens*) and parsley (*Petroselinum crispum*) for Black Swallowtails; hops (*Humulus lupulus*) for anglewings and Red Admirals; borage (*Borago officinalis*) for Painted Ladies; sweet violet (*Viola odorata*) for fritillaries.

Nectar-Rich Herbs for Butterflies

Agastache foeniculum Anise hyssop	*Origanum vulgare* Oregano, wild marjoram
Echinacea species Coneflowers	*Pycnanthemum* species Mountain mints
Hyssopus officinalis Hyssop	*Rosmarinus officinalis* Rosemary
Inula helenium Elecampane	*Salvia* species Sages
Lavandula species and hybrids Lavenders	*Satureja hortensis* Summer savory
Mentha species and hybrids Mints	*Taraxacum officinale* Dandelion
Monarda species Bee balms	*Thymus* species and hybrids Thymes
Ocimum basilicum Basil	*Tropaeolum majus* Nasturtium

Herbs That Feed Caterpillars

Anethum graveolens Dill . . . . .Black Swallowtail, Anise Swallowtail

Artemisia dracunculus Russian tarragon . . . . .Swallowtails

Asclepias tuberosa Butterfly weed . . . . .Monarch

Dictamnus albus Burning bush . . . . .Giant Swallowtail

Foeniculum vulgare Fennel . . . . .Anise Swallowtail

Glycyrrhiza species Licorice . . . . .Silver-Spotted Skipper

Humulus lupulus Hops . . . . .Gray Hairstreak, Question Mark, Red Admiral

Levisticum officinale Lovage . . . . .Black Swallowtail, Anise Swallowtail

Petroselinum crispum Parsley . . . . .Black Swallowtail, Anise Swallowtail

Pimpinella anisum Anise .Black Swallowtail, Anise Swallowtail

Populus balsamifera Balsam poplar . . .White Admiral, Viceroy, Western Tiger Swallowtail

Rumex acetosella Sheep sorrel . . . . .Little Copper

Ruta graveolens Rue . . . . .Black Swallowtail, Giant Swallowtail

Tropaeolum majus Nasturtium . . . . .Cabbage White

Urtica dioica Nettle . . . . .Milbert's Tortoiseshell, Red Admiral

Viburnum lentago Nannyberry . . . . .Spring Azure

Viola odorata Sweet violet . . . . .Fritillaries

You can also include herbal trees, such as balsam poplar (*Populus balsamifera*), host for White Admirals and Western Tiger Swallowtails; or large shrubs like nannyberry (*Viburnum lentago*) and witch-hazel (*Hamamelis virginiana*) for Spring Azures. Even herbal groundcovers can host caterpillars: wintergreen (*Gaultheria procumbens*) for Baltimores; wild strawberry (*Fragaria virginiana*) for Gray Hairstreaks.

The love of sunshine is something that herbs and butterflies have in common. Think about adding a sun-drenched brick or stone pathway that sets off herbs and provides countless niches for creeping thyme (*Thymus praecox* var. *arcticus* or *Thymus serpyllum*), chamomile, and other low growers. Butterflies, which are ectothermic, use the sunny stones as basking spots. Let the path meander, and make it wide enough for the lanky stems of lavender to droop over the edge.

How much backyard gardening actually supports butterfly populations is unclear; however, every effort helps. Your herb garden can become a valuable tool for teaching children and adults about the joys of observing these colorful insects.

How to Grow a Butterfly Gardener

Sharon Lovejoy

My earliest memories of childhood are entwined with the flashing wings of butterflies and the brilliant flowers of my grandmother's sunny, old-fashioned garden. The hidden world behind our fragrant privet hedge always seemed more alive and enchanted than any other yard in the neighborhood.

Why was it that the dark, velvety Mourning Cloaks landed on me as though I were a flower? What made the yellow-and-black swallowtails spend so much time on the ferny-leafed fennel plants? Was the Common Buckeye watching my every move from those six big eyes that bordered its fawn-colored wings?

Those and other questions, and the foundation that magical garden provided, turned me into a passionate, lifelong butterfly enthusiast and gardener with a mission to share that passion with children. In 1986, that dream came true in a tiny community garden my family planted in the heart of our village. The goal was to inspire and educate children with our garden, but instead the children became the inspiration and teachers, educating me about what worked for them. They reminded me that all knowledge is first rooted in wonder, and that wonder is one of the most important components of gardening.

I read nearly every available book on butterfly gardening before planting the first beds and borders. The books offered a standard array of simple requirements for a successful garden, and most emphasized that the design was of secondary, if any, importance. But, in a child's garden, the element of design should be moved to the

Getting close to butterflies is fun, especially for children. Above, a Monarch butterfly feasts on purple coneflower, *Echinacea purpurea*.

top of the list. I learned this the hard way after planting dozens of flowers in wide, exuberant beds. The youngsters who visited my gardens wanted a close-up view of the coppery, spangled Monarchs feeding from the pineapple sage (*Salvia elegans*) in the center of the beds and didn't understand the traditional boundaries. The temptation was too great, and the flower beds became footpaths, shortcuts to where the action was. In the process of getting close to the butterflies, the children trampled everything in their path.

For me, the lesson was clear; children want and need to be immersed in the myriad natural rhythms of the garden. Constant reprimands or signs that warn them not to touch anything would defeat the purpose of a garden especially created for children. After all, I wanted to grow a new generation of butterfly gardeners, not merely a splashy display of perfect flowers.

Attracting Children and Butterflies

If your dream is to plant a butterfly garden for your children, you'll need to look at your yard from the viewpoint of both child and butterfly. Think small, and create garden beds that are suited to the children's size, so that your time together outdoors is spent enjoying the butterflies, not doing chores. Think abundance, and crowd troupes of nectar-rich plants together for the ultimate one-stop sipping spot. Think future,

In a garden with wide paths and relatively small beds, children can move in on the action without causing butterfly or plant casualties.

and include caterpillar host plants to nourish the next generation of butterflies. Think native, and place a copse or hedgerow of indigenous butterfly plants somewhere in your yard to provide both food and shelter. Think easy-to-grow, and plant species that aren't plagued by disease or that may self-sow for a repeat performance.

Forget about the ideal of a "picture perfect" garden and let things become a bit raggle-taggle. A few dead leaves and stalks provide winter homes for some species of butterflies, like the cosmopolitan Painted Ladies, which overwinter as chrysalides attached to stalks or branches. Lose your aversion to bugs, slugs, and other garden thugs whose appearance might make you want to launch into a deadly spray or bait campaign. Neither children nor butterflies should ever be exposed to poisons. Finally, consider designing your beds in a shape that will encircle your children and allow them to be in the heart of the garden without doing either the plants or the butter-flies any harm.

Creating a Child-Friendly Butterfly Environment

Provided that you pick a sunny and sheltered area—two ingredients necessary for solar-powered butterflies to prosper—you have many options for designing a butter-fly garden that's inviting to children. Any shape that allows easy plant access, such as a crescent, an open rectangle, or an elongated horseshoe shape works well. A large (ten-foot by ten-foot) butterfly with outstretched wings got the most enthusiastic response from the children in our community garden. To provide access, the "body," or center of the bed, is intersected by a three-foot pathway of flat paving stones and interplanted with a nonflowering chamomile (*Chamaemelum nobile* 'Treneague') that wafts the scent of apples when trod upon. To prevent possible bee stings or butterfly casualties, it's safest to avoid interplanting the pathway with flowering species.

No matter what shape you choose, prepare the garden beds as you would for any planting, but add a border of rocks or other suitable materials to define the shape, then fill the interior of the beds with good topsoil and mulch. Add extra soil in the center of each bed to form an elevated mound.

Most books caution against overplanting or crowding beds and borders, but a sunny butterfly garden in good soil with a blanket of mulch and a regimen of organic fertilizers is an exception. Think of your garden as a flowery welcome mat for butterflies—the more blooms, the more bounty and the bigger the crowds. The added bonus is that the dense planting helps to keep down weeds.

In a perfect scenario, something is always in bloom to tantalize and nurture the

---

Simple Ways to Enhance the Garden for Children and Butterflies

- Take photos of the children in the garden and photograph the entire process, from the first bare outline of the design through the bountiful days of summer and autumn. Keep photos, drawings, memorable quotes, and notes in a nature journal you create together.

- Set some flat rocks in sunny areas throughout the garden for a great opportunity to observe butterflies at rest. Cold-blooded critters, butterflies need to warm their muscles before they can fly and will bask on the solar collecting slabs for long periods.

- Fill a saucer with sand and soil and moisten it slightly, then let the children add a little table salt to the mixture before setting it outdoors. Butterflies in search of minerals will linger and sip at the saucer.

- Fill a saucer with thin slices of watermelon, which is as sweet a taste treat for butterflies as it is for children, and set it in the garden.

- Mix 1/3 cup of sugar with a cup of water, and stir it thoroughly. Set some colorful (and clean) pink, yellow, and purple sponges, or pieces of sponge, in a saucer, and cover them with the sugar syrup until they are soaked. Place the saucer in a favorite butterfly haunt outside. Clean the sponges in hot—but not soapy—water every few days to prevent mold.

- Purchase an inexpensive plastic magnifying glass and tether it to a slender pole near the garden so children can closely view feeding butterflies and the intricacies of every flower blossom.

See the box "Rearing Butterfly Caterpillars," page 45, for another butterfly project.

butterflies through the entire growing season. Refer to the labels on nursery plants, and check the "Encyclopedia of Butterfly and Caterpillar Plants," page 67, to learn about flowering times, then select a medley of robust annuals and perennials that will flaunt their blooms without a lot of coddling.

Use a stair-step approach when you arrange the plants, working from the top of the mound to the outer borders. Tuck the loftiest specimens, such as Mexican sunflowers (*Tithonia*), sunflowers (*Helianthus*), or the wandlike *Verbena bonariensis* atop the highest point, and follow with descending steps of shorter species, such as asters and sedums, which bloom into autumn, coneflowers (*Echinacea*), catmint (*Nepeta*), heliotrope (*Heliotropium*), and pincushion flowers (*Scabiosa*), one of the seductive stars of the butterfly garden. (Note: *Verbena bonariensis* is being monitored as a potentially invasive plant in Washington State. For more information, visit www.wa.gov/agr/weedboard.) Finish the edges of the borders with a lacy collar of fleabane (*Erigeron*), ground-hugging thymes (*Thymus*), alyssums, pinks (*Dianthus*), or yarrows (*Achillea*). Look closely once these borders are established, and you'll discover another world of often overlooked butterflies: the tiny hairstreaks, elusive blues, skippers, and metalmarks.

Containers, the great quick-change artists of any garden, are a simple way to add another dimension to the design. Station one or more in sunny areas throughout the butterfly garden, and fill them with a colorful, seasonal parade of nectar-rich blooming annuals, such as cosmos, miniature sunflowers (*Helianthus annuus* 'Teddy Bear', 'Elf', 'Sunspot', or 'Music Box Mix'), and marigolds (*Tagetes*).

If you choose to design the giant butterfly, place a large pot at the top of each forewing in the antenna area and crown it with a simple willow or wire-work tepee. Tuck in some of the caterpillar host plants of the most common butterflies in your neighborhood, and wait for the show to begin. The females will cruise past your offerings, settle on individual host-plant leaves, and "taste" them with their tarsi (feet) to determine suitability for their offspring. If the match is correct, they may stay, allowing the children to experience egg-laying, hatching, and development of the voracious caterpillars firsthand.

Every day you spend together outdoors with the butterflies and flowers will underscore the wisdom of the old adage that "more grows in a garden than is planted." In an alchemy as magical as the transformation that brews inside a chrysalis, children exposed to such a place will metamorphose into the caring naturalists and wildlife gardeners of the future.

Encyclopedia of Butterfly and Caterpillar Plants

Northeast

Jane Ruffin

About 50 butterfly species have visited my suburban garden in southeastern Pennsylvania. Although the area is densely populated, the neighborhood has a good mix of mature trees and a stream. Tiger, Black, and Spicebush Swallowtails are spotted every year.

When I created a butterfly garden in the front yard of our three-quarter-acre lot, some of my neighbors were a little surprised. Lawn and shade trees in the front are the American way of life in the suburbs, but in my garden, butterfly plants are crammed together cottage-garden style. I am happy to say that people now stop to look at the flowers and butterflies, and several of my neighbors have followed my example.

The front garden peaks in early summer, with blooming perennials, including native wildflowers and grasses, ornamental onions, salvias, and other herbs. They are set against native shrubs, such as azaleas; leadplant (*Amorpha fruticosa*), a host for the Silver-Spotted Skipper; snowberry (*Symphoricarpus orbiculatus*) and arrowwood (*Viburnum dentatum*), hosts for two species of hummingbird moths; as well as sweet pepperbush (*Clethra alnifolia*) and other viburnums, which are wonderful nectar sources.

Later in the season mountain mints (*Pycnanthemum*), purple coneflower (*Echinacea purpurea*), joe-pye weed (*Eupatorium fistulosum*), boneset (*E. perfoliatum*), ironweed (*Vernonia noveboracensis*), and low-growing goldenrods (*Solidago*), all good nectar plants, take over. Mountain mints attract small butterflies, such as blues and hairstreaks. One morning I had the pleasure of watching one Striped Hairstreak, with several Red-Banded and Banded Hairstreaks, nectaring at the flowers.

The backyard faces north and has mature trees underplanted with spring-flowering bulbs, viburnums, hollies (*Ilex*), and native and nonnative azaleas. I also have some volunteer hackberries (*Celtis occidentalis*), sassafras (*Sassafras albidum*), and

Red-Spotted Purples, common butterflies in the Northeast.

spicebush (*Lindera benzoin*). When the weather warms I add impatiens, salvias, and bee balm (*Monarda didyma*), which lasts about three years in the shade, at which point it can be replaced from plants in full sun that have outgrown their spot. They produce fewer large flowers in the shade, but they last a little longer than those in the full sun. Many of the butterflies' favorite flowers are good for hummingbirds, too.

I cut back the hackberries very hard, and some of them are beginning to look quite interesting. The trunk of one of them is about four inches in diameter. The bark is ridged, making it a striking winter tree. Question Marks, Hackberry Emperors, and Snouts all laid eggs on the new leaves.

My west-facing garden blooms in the fall. Three red cedars and more viburnums form the background for this garden. I live in the hope of a Juniper Hairstreak finding her way to my garden, laying eggs on the red cedar, and starting a colony! The rest of the space is full of native white, lavender, and purple asters and late-flowering salvias that bloom until frost. The salvias come in amazing colors—dark red, indigo blue, purple, and more—and the hummingbirds set up territories as the flowers increase. Monarchs, Red-Spotted Purples, American Ladies, and commas are usually found here on a daily basis. As the sun goes down, the flowers are all backlit, making a sensational autumn display.

I leave the gardens alone until late March. In spring I cut back to the ground nearly everything and weed out unwanted plants or share them with friends and neighbors.

Host Plants for Caterpillars

Aristolochia macrophylla (*A. durior*) Dutchman's Pipe

Deciduous vine excellent for making a screen or cover. Small green and yellow "pipe"-shaped flowers. Established plants may grow to 30 feet.

Native Habitat Woods, streambanks from Pennsylvania to Georgia and Kansas

Hardiness Zones 5 to 8

Aristolochia durior, **Dutchman's pipe.**

Blooming Period May to June

Growing Tips Rich soil, sun or part shade. Provide a strong support for vines.

Caterpillars Hosted Pipevine Swallowtail

Butterflies Attracted None known (or likely, as the plant is fly-pollinated)

Asclepias incarnata Swamp Milkweed

Perennial plant with milky sap, clusters of pink and white blossoms. A beautiful white cultivar 'Ice Ballet' is available. Height is 3 to 5 feet.

Native Habitat Wet places from Nova Scotia to South Carolina

Hardiness Zones 4 to 8

Blooming Period June and July. If it flowers early, deadhead and it may flower again.

Growing Tips Full sun, average to moist soil. Yellow aphids can be controlled by spraying a jet of water or hand rubbing.

Caterpillars Hosted Monarch

Butterflies Attracted Excellent nectar source for many butterfly species

Ceanothus americanus New Jersey Tea

Compact shrub to 4 feet with dark green leaves and clusters of tiny white flowers

Native Habitat Dry, open woods, rocky banks, southern Pennsylvania to Texas

Hardiness Zones 7 to 8

Blooming Period June

Growing Tips Likes sun and light, well-drained soil. In hard winters will die back, but new growth comes from the ground.

Caterpillars Hosted Spring Azure

Butterflies Attracted Spring butterflies, such as blues

Salix discolor • Pussy willow

Bushy shrub or small tree to 20 feet. Narrow-leafed, with yellow blossoms that form on silvery catkins.

Native Habitat Moist areas from Labrador to Kentucky, west through the Plains states to the Rockies

Hardiness Zones 4 to 8

Blooming Period Early spring

Growing Tips Moist soil, sun

Caterpillars Hosted Mourning Cloak, Red-Spotted Purple, Viceroy

Butterflies Attracted Mourning Cloak

Sulphur on *Aster novae-angliae*, New England aster.

Vaccinium angustifolium
Lowbush blueberry

Bushy deciduous shrub to 3 feet with small white flowers and edible fruit

Native Habitat Open woods, upland ridges from Nova Scotia to Georgia and Missouri

Hardiness Zones 4 to 8

Blooming Period April to May

Growing Tips Flourishes in both sun and light shade. Adapted to dry soil.

Caterpillars Hosted Spring Azure, Brown Elfin

Butterflies Attracted Early butterflies, such as blues

Zizia aurea • Golden Alexanders

Compound-leaf perennial, 1 to 2½ feet high, in the parsley family with umbels of tiny yellow flowers.

Native Habitat Meadows, open woods, streamsides from New Brunswick to Florida and Texas

Hardiness Zones 4 to 9

Blooming Period May to June

Growing Tips Moist, rich soil in part sun

Caterpillars Hosted Black Swallowtail

Butterflies Attracted Early-season butterflies such as blues, and many others

Nectar Plants for Butterflies

Aster novae-angliae (*Symphyotrichum novae-angliae*) • New England Aster

Clusters of rose, pink, and violet flowers with yellow eyes growing to 4 or 5 feet tall. The tough plants bring a final flush of color to the autumn garden.

Native Habitat Damp thickets and wet meadows from New England to Alabama, westward to North Dakota and Wyoming

Hardiness Zones 3 to 9

Blooming Period Late summer and fall

Growing Tips Grow in full sun and moist soil. To avoid staking and produce bushier plants, prune growing tips in early summer.

Butterflies Attracted Sulphurs, Pearl Crescent, American Lady, Monarch. Host to Pearl Crescent caterpillars.

Eupatorium coelestinum, mistflower.

Eupatorium coelestinum (Conoclinium coelestinum) Mistflower, Hardy Ageratum

Upright stems 2 to 3 feet tall topped with flat-topped, fluffy clusters of powder-blue flowers.

Native Habitat Wet meadows, low woods, and roadside ditches from New Jersey to Missouri south to Florida and Texas

Hardiness Zones 4 to 9

Blooming Period Late summer and fall

Growing Tips Plant in full sun to partial shade in moist to wet soil; tolerates poor drainage. Spreads readily by rhizome and may require frequent division to keep it under control.

Butterflies Attracted Sulphurs, skippers, Monarch

Lilium superbum • Turk's Cap Lily

A spectacular lily 3 to 8 feet tall, with orange to red-orange, strongly reflexed flowers

Native Habitat Wet meadows and swamp edges from New Hampshire and Massachusetts south to Alabama and Georgia

Hardiness Zones 4 to 9

Blooming Period Summer

Growing Tips One of the easiest native lilies to cultivate. Prefers moist to wet soil in sun or part sun.

Butterflies Attracted Eastern Tiger Swallowtail, Spicebush Swallowtail, Silver-Spotted Skipper

Pycnanthemum muticum Mountain Mint

A handsome species about 3 feet tall, with gray-green leaves and well-developed bracts surrounding the flower heads. Casts a silvery haze over the late-summer garden.

Native Habitat Moist woods, thickets, and fields from Massachusetts to Michigan south to Florida and Louisiana

Pycnanthemum muticum, mountain mint.

Monarchs on *Solidago sempervirens*, seaside goldenrod.

Hardiness Zones 3 to 9

Blooming Period Midsummer to frost

Growing Tips Easy to grow in average soil in a sunny or partially sunny spot. Spreads enthusiastically on long rhizomes, so give it room to ramble.

Butterflies Attracted All small butterflies, including Gray Hairstreak, Red-Banded Hairstreak, Eastern Tailed-Blue, Spring Azure

Solidago sempervirens
Seaside Goldenrod

A robust plant 2 to 4 feet tall, with fleshy leaves and thick panicles of bright golden-yellow flowers with curving side branches.

Native Habitat Sandy soils and dunes along the East Coast, from Newfoundland to the Gulf states

Hardiness Zones 4 to 7

Blooming Period Late August through September

Growing Tips Prefers poor, sandy, well-drained soil in sun

Butterflies Attracted Monarch, Juniper Hairstreak, Sachem, Silver-Spotted Skipper. Host to Baltimore, Silvery Checkerspot caterpillars.

Viburnum dentatum • Arrowwood

A treelike or multistemmed deciduous shrub growing to 15 feet tall. Abundant clusters of creamy white flowers appear in late spring. Clusters of dark blue fruits ripen from late August to November. Lustrous, toothed leaves turn yellow to salmon to reddish purple in fall.

Native Habitat Moist, low ground along streams and in thickets

Hardiness Zones 2 to 8

Blooming Period Late spring

Growing Tips Grow in moist, sandy loam in full sun to partial shade.

Butterflies Attracted Red Admiral, Eastern Comma, Question Mark. Host to hummingbird moth caterpillars.

Southeast

Kim Hawks

My interest in butterflies snuck up on me while I was creating a wildflower nursery in Chapel Hill, North Carolina. After several years of building up our selections of perennials native to the Southeast, I began incorporating these plants in display gardens. The nursery and gardens have open, bright light, and are surrounded by a mixed hardwood and pine forest. The gardens have grown to encompass approximately an acre.

Many southern gardens are heavy on spring color, then turn predominantly green in the heat of summer, relying on seasonal annuals for summer and fall color. Using native perennials, I chose to create a garden bursting with summer color that crescendos in the fall. I wanted to show a more relaxed, informal, and colorful way to design and garden, creating healthy habitats that are beautiful.

I began by creating a variety of irregular island beds using shrubs and perennials. Each island bed has a name relating to the theme of that space. In one sunny area, I created a Meadow Giants garden approximately forty feet long by fifteen feet wide. This garden includes summer-blooming native perennials that grow to four feet or taller, such as several species of *Rudbeckia*, *Helianthus*, *Monarda*, *Eupatorium*, and *Liatris*, along with asters, phlox, and goldenrods (*Solidago*). I watched this garden quickly grow into a tapestry of mixed-green textures, then, like fireworks, burst into bloom from July until late fall. In the first season of planting, seemingly out of nowhere, butterflies and birds magically appeared. Wow! I decided to intentionally make the display garden an oasis for these lovely creatures.

The Hot Colors border features red, burgundy, gold, yellow, and orange blooms, with a little blue thrown in. Indian blanket (*Gaillardia pulchella*), oxeye daisy (*Heliopsis helianthoides*), and several species of *Rudbeckia* provide nectar for many butterflies.

Many southern gardens lack summer and fall flowers that butterflies like this Tiger Swallowtail need.

In the White Border that flanks the entry drive, butterflies flock to the compact flowers of white coneflower (*Echinacea purpurea* 'Kim's Mop Head') and to the summer-blooming white flowers of *Verbena canadensis* 'Alba'. Mountain mint (*Pycnanthemum incanum*) offers multilayered tiers of silvery white blooms with nectar relished by an incredible assortment of butterflies and other insects.

The Medicinal Garden showcases native medicinal plants, such as purple coneflower (*Echinacea purpurea*), passion-vine (*Passiflora incarnata*), red bee balm (*Monarda didyma*), and Culver's root (*Veronicastrum virginicum*). All of these plants provide nectar for a variety of butterflies.

In the Woodland Garden, several shrubs lure butterflies, including compact sweet pepperbush (*Clethra alnifolia* 'Hummingbird'), red buckeye (*Aesculus pavia*), and strawberry bush, or heart's a burstin' (*Euonymus americanus*).

Throughout the garden, dozens of Tiger Swallowtails hover around the joe-pye weed (*Eupatorium fistulosum*), which is my hands-down favorite butterfly magnet. Flurries of Monarchs sip the nectar of the vibrant orange flowers of butterfly weed (*Asclepias tuberosa*). Question Marks nectar on various aster species.

Larval host plants in the garden include passion-vine for Gulf Fritillaries, sassafras (*Sassafras albidum*) for Spicebush Swallowtails, and Virginia snakeroot (*Aristolochia serpentaria*) for Pipevine Swallowtails.

The gardens peak in the fall with many fall-blooming flowers, such as goldenrods, asters, salvias, and gayfeathers (*Liatris*). Our gardens continue to lure butterflies throughout the autumn.

Host Plants for Caterpillars

Baptisia australis • False Indigo

Like other baptisias, a rugged, long-lived, drought-tolerant perennial. Magnificent bluish-purple pea-shaped flowers in spring on 3-foot by 3-foot mounded plants, complemented by blue-green cloverlike leaves.

Native Habitat Prairies and open woodland areas from New York to Nebraska south to Texas and Georgia

Hardiness Zones 3 to 9

Blooming Period Mid- to late spring

Growing Tips Thriving in full sun and average to dry soils, it spends the first two to three years establishing a deep taproot, then matures into a lovely plant bearing numerous spikes of spring color.

Caterpillars Hosted Orange Sulphur, Clouded Sulphur, Frosted Elfin, Eastern Tailed-Blue, Hoary Edge, Wild Indigo Duskywing

Butterflies Attracted None known

Alternate Choice *Baptisia alba*, white false indigo

Cercis canadensis • Eastern Redbud

A 20- to 30-foot understory tree producing rosy-pink, purplish flowers on bare branches in early spring, followed by heart-shaped leaves. A lovely plant for the edge of woodland areas or in sun. Concurrently blooms with flowering dogwood (*Cornus florida*).

Native Habitat New Jersey to northern Florida west to Missouri and Texas and northern Mexico

Hardiness Zones 4 to 9

Blooming Period Early spring

Growing Tips Sun to part shade, moist soil

Caterpillars Hosted Henry's Elfin

Butterflies Attracted Early butterflies such as blues; also bees, hummingbirds

Chelone glabra • White Turtlehead

Makes moist woodland gardens come alive in late summer when its white "turtle-head" flowers come into bloom. Over time, 3- to 4-foot plants form colonies. A great companion to cardinal flower (*Lobelia cardinalis*).

Native Habitat Newfoundland to Minnesota south to Alabama and Georgia in wet woodland areas

Hardiness Zones 3 to 9

Blooming Period Late summer

Growing Tips Plant in semishade, in rich, moist soil. Clumps spread rapidly.

Caterpillars Hosted Baltimore

Butterflies Attracted Silver-Spotted Skipper, Spicebush Swallowtail, Eastern Tiger Swallowtail

Alternate Choice *Chelone lyonii,* pink turtlehead

Panicum virgatum • Switchgrass

A clumping grass growing to 6 feet tall. In the fall, light, airy panicles may open

Baptisia australis, false indigo.

Monarch on *Vernonia noveboracensis,* New York ironweed.

reddish pink. Texturally, offers a light effect with movement in the wind.

Native Habitat Prairies, open fields, open woods, and marshy areas from eastern Canada through the U.S., except along the Pacific Coast.

Hardiness Zones 4 to 9

Blooming Period Fall to winter

Growing Tips Adapts to a wide range of sunny conditions. Thrives in areas that are periodically wet as well as well-drained sites, and in heavy clay soils as well as sandy sites. Drought-tolerant once established.

Caterpillars Hosted Least Skipper, Tawny-Edged Skipper, Northern Broken-Dash, Delaware Skipper

Butterflies Attracted None known (or likely, as the plant is wind-pollinated and produces no nectar)

Solidago rugosa
Rough-Leafed Goldenrod

A lacy dome of golden flowers appears on 3- to 5-foot-tall perennials with coarse leaves and stems.

Native Habitat Roadsides, fields from Newfoundland to Michigan south to Texas and Florida

Hardiness Zones 4 to 9

Blooming Period Late summer to early fall

Growing Tips Plant in full sun in lean soil and give it plenty of room to grow. Stake if necessary.

Caterpillars Hosted Baltimore, Silvery Checkerspot

Butterflies Attracted Monarch, American Lady, swallowtails

Vernonia noveboracensis
New York Ironweed

Intense purple blooms appear in late summer on 6- to 8-foot leafy stems. Plant this strong, dependable, drought-tolerant native in the rear of the border; it looks great with fall-blooming goldenrods and sunflowers.

Native Habitat Open fields, ditches, and marshy areas from Massachusetts to Pennsylvania south to Florida and Alabama

Hardiness Zones 4 to 8

Blooming Period Late summer

Growing Tips Grows in sun to light shade in both poorly drained or well-drained soils.

Caterpillars Hosted American Lady

Butterflies Attracted Many, including swallowtails, Monarch, American Lady

Nectar Plants for Butterflies

Clethra alnifolia • **Sweet Pepperbush**

A deciduous shrub to about 8 feet tall. Produces sweetly scented spikes of white, sometimes light pink flowers in summer. The leaves turn brilliant yellow in autumn.

Native Habitat Swampy areas throughout eastern North America

Hardiness Zones 4 to 10

Blooming Period Late July and August

Growing Tips Prefers full sun to partial shade and moist, well-drained soil; tolerates wet soils.

Butterflies Attracted Many, including swallowtails, Silver-Spotted Skipper

Echinacea purpurea **Purple Coneflower**

A robust perennial 2 to 4 feet tall. Flower heads consist of dozens of daisies with dark rose, rarely white rays (petals) around a central orange-brown cone.

Native Habitat Prairies, meadows, and forest gaps from Michigan and Virginia south to Louisiana and Georgia

Hardiness Zones 3 to 8

Blooming Period Summer

Growing Tips Easy to grow in full sun or part shade. Deadheading encourages continued flower production. Many cultivars are available.

Butterflies Attracted Many, including swallowtails, hairstreaks, Viceroy

Eupatorium fistulosum, joe-pye weed.

Eupatorium fistulosum • **Joe-pye Weed**

A giant plant with straight stems 6 to 14 feet tall, crowned by huge domes of dusty mauve, sometimes white or red-purple flowers.

Native Habitat Wet meadows and forest openings from Maine to Iowa south to Florida and Texas

Hardiness Zones 4 to 9

Blooming Period Late summer

Growing Tips Grow in moist to wet soil in sun or part sun. Established plants need little attention.

Butterflies Attracted Many, including Painted Lady, Eastern Tiger Swallowtail

Helianthus angustifolius **Swamp Sunflower**

A stately beauty with 4- to 8-foot stems covered with deep green, lance-shaped leaves. Large numbers of black-eyed daisies with yellow rays (petals) are borne on the upper quarter of each stem.

Native Habitat Coastal swamps and wet meadows from New York south to the Gulf states

Hardiness Zones 5 to 9

Blooming Period Autumn

Growing Tips Prefers sun or part sun and moist to wet soil.

Butterflies Attracted Painted Lady, Red Admiral, Monarch. Host to American Lady caterpillars.

Hibiscus moscheutos • Rose Mallow

Dramatic, shrublike perennial, 4 to 7 feet tall, with 6-to 8-inch red-centered flowers crowding the upper parts of the stems. Although plants in the wild typically have white flowers, darker pink-flowered cultivars are the most commonly cultivated.

Native Habitat Wet meadows, low woods, marshes, and roadside ditches from Massachusetts to Wisconsin south to Florida and Texas

Hardiness Zones 4 to 9

Blooming Period Late summer

Growing Tips Plant in evenly moist, humus-rich soil in full sun or light shade. Space plants at least 3 feet apart because they dislike being transplanted.

Butterflies Attracted Gulf Fritillary, Eastern Tiger Swallowtail, blues, hairstreaks

Rudbeckia laciniata, ragged coneflower.

Rudbeckia laciniata • Ragged Coneflower, Cutleaf Coneflower

A big, free-flowering summer bloomer bearing a multitude of flowers with drooping, lemon-yellow rays (petals) surrounding green cones.

Native Habitat Streamsides and other moist sites from Quebec and Montana south to Florida and Arizona

Hardiness Zones 3 to 9

Blooming Period Summer

Growing Tips Prefers rich, moist soil in sun or part shade.

Butterflies Attracted Fritillaries, blues, Viceroy, Monarch. Host to Silvery Checkerspot caterpillars.

Hibiscus moscheutos, rose mallow.

Florida

Pamela F. Traas

A brilliant flash of a butterfly's wings as it flits through my garden holds me spellbound for a moment. Just as quickly it is gone. Unfortunately, with the rapid disappearance of butterfly habitat in fast-developing Florida, these chance encounters are happening with less and less frequency.

To lend butterflies a helping hand, I decided to join the growing ranks of local butterfly fanciers and create a butterfly sanctuary on my 50- by 150-foot lot. Along the way, I discovered a dizzying array of native plants that feed and shelter these beautiful creatures.

I live in a small, sleepy town nestled on the banks of Old Tampa Bay, in central Florida. My house is just four blocks from Main Street and four blocks from the bay. The neighborhood has redbrick streets and is filled with an eclectic mix of funky old (1919) front-porch cottages, elegant town homes, and a smattering of small apartment complexes. In true Florida fashion, I have decorated my front yard with pink flamingos and large butterflies that are strung with lights.

My yard is a certified butterfly sanctuary and wildlife habitat. My next-door neighbor is encouraging the passion-vine (*Passiflora*) that has crept under his fence, and I have shared plants and cuttings with many local gardeners. Butterfly gardens are sprouting up everywhere.

In my area we have also been on an enforced, once-a-week watering restriction for the last few years. One of the beauties of growing native plants is that once they have been established, their water requirements are minimal.

When we first moved into our house, we removed sand spurs and any trace of grass from the front yard and replaced them with a butterfly garden—a small wild area with stepping-stone paths surrounded by a colorful mix of native and nonnative

In fast-developing Florida, habitat for butterflies like this Zebra Heliconian is disappearing rapidly.

plants. There is always something in bloom, and the butterflies, moths, bees, wasps, and beetles love it.

In my backyard, the fence is covered with vines: passion-vines, pipevines (*Aristolochia*), American wisteria (*Wisteria frutescens*), and trumpet creeper (*Campsis radicans*) among them. I grow more than 50 pots of various butterfly plants.

The many caterpillar host plants I supply include passion-vines for Gulf Fritillaries and Zebra Heliconians, wild lime (*Zanthoxylum fagara*) for Giant Swallowtails, and a lovely red bay tree (*Persea borbonia*) for Spicebush Swallowtails.

Blessed with year-round butterfly activity, the challenge has been to learn the rhythm of the broods, then provide a constant source of food both for the caterpillars and the adults. For instance, I get a heavy influx of Monarchs usually in late March and again in early December. I don't see any Black Swallowtails until mid- to late summer, yet the Gulf Fritillaries seem to have a new brood every three weeks, all year.

When I step out my back door, it is into a whirlwind of activity. Depending on the time of year, Monarchs, Gulf Fritillaries, Zebras, duskywings, sulphurs, and swallowtails are everywhere. My butterfly garden not only replaces a bit of precious habitat but also keeps alive the childlike wonder in me.

Passiflora incarnata, **passion-vine.**

Host Plants for Caterpillars

Chamaecrista fasciculata
Partridge Pea

A compact annual wildflower that will grow as wide as it is tall, usually up to 3 feet. Produces reddish stems and bright yellow, five-petal blossoms that cover the feathery foliage.

Native Habitat Widely varied, including sandhill, scrub, pine flatwoods, dunes, open hammocks, and disturbed areas

Hardiness Zones 5 to 11

Blooming Period Spring through fall

Growing Tips Plant in sandy, well-drained soil; full sun. Reseeds freely.

Caterpillars Hosted Cloudless Sulphur, Little Yellow, Ceraunus Blue, and Gray Hairstreak

Butterflies Attracted None known

Passiflora incarnata
Passion-Vine, Maypop

A vigorous perennial vine with three-lobed leaves and long red stems, best known for the stunning purple and white flowers that cover it, and for the edible fruit it produces.

Native Habitat Sand hills, disturbed areas

Hardiness Zones 6 to 11

Blooming Period Spring, summer, and into fall

Growing Tips Take cuttings or dig root suckers in spring and plant in well-drained soil in full sun with plenty of room to roam. Can be grown from seeds, but they are very slow to germinate. This is an aggressive vine that can take over your garden; however, in colder climates it will die back to the roots in the winter.

Caterpillars Hosted Zebra Heliconian, Julia Heliconian, Gulf Fritillary, and Variegated Fritillary

Butterflies Attracted None known

Persea borbonia • Red Bay

Lovely medium-size evergreen tree that rarely tops 40 feet. Large aromatic, dark green leaves are edible. Round, dark blue fruits that ripen in the fall follow the inconspicuous yellow flowers that bloom in small clusters in spring.

Native Habitat Upland forests and coastal hammocks along the coast from southern Delaware to eastern Louisiana, including all of Florida except the Keys

Hardiness Zones 7 to 10

Blooming Period Spring

Growing Tips Will grow from seed; potted specimens are available at most nurseries. Plant ripe seeds in sandy to rich soil in a sunny area with room to grow. Affected by leaf gall; it doesn't harm the tree, but can detract from the beauty of the specimen.

Caterpillars Hosted Spicebush and Palamedes Swallowtails

Butterflies Attracted None known

Phyla nodiflora • Matchhead, Creeping Charlie, Fog Fruit

Considered a common lawn weed, matchhead is an excellent evergreen perennial groundcover that rarely grows above 6 inches. Will form a dense mat with tiny purple-tinged white flowers that ring the end of its compact head, giving it the appearance of a match.

Native Habitat Varies widely from wet areas to sandy hiking paths, coastal dunes, marshes, and disturbed areas

Hardiness Zones 5 to 11

Blooming Period Year-round; spring to frost in the northern part of the state

Growing Tips Rarely found in nurseries, but very common and easily propagated. Reproduces by seed and by sending out shoots that root at the nodes. Plant a well-rooted cutting in full sun to partial shade in average or sandy soil.

Caterpillars Hosted Phoan Crescent, Common Buckeye

Butterflies Attracted Almost all of Florida's butterflies, including White Peacock, Great Southern White, Checkered White, Gulf Fritillary, Common Buckeye, Phoan and Pearl Crescents, many skippers, and blues

Phyla nodiflora, matchhead.

Plumbago scandens • Wild Plumbago

A wonderful semiwoody shrub that sprawls, forming tangled mounds to 5 feet tall. This evergreen perennial is covered all year with small white flowers borne on spikes that shower gracefully downward.

Native Habitat Coastal hammocks, shell mounds

Hardiness Zones 8 to 11

Blooming Period Year-round

Growing Tips Easily propagated by cuttings or division at a rooted node. Plant in full sun to partial shade in sandy, well-drained, alkaline soil.

Caterpillars Hosted Cassius Blue. Look for the caterpillars in the seedpods and flowers.

Butterflies Attracted Cassius Blue

Zanthoxylum fagara • Wild Lime

A small evergreen tree with fragrant compound leaves, spiky thorns on bark and stems, and tiny, greenish-yellow flowers.

Native Habitat Coastal hammocks, shell mounds

Hardiness Zones 9 to 11

Blooming Period Late spring, early summer

Growing Tips Plant in full sun to partial shade in well-drained, sandy soil. Grows very fast and will self-sow. Available at many Florida native nurseries.

Caterpillars Hosted Giant Swallowtail, Schaus Swallowtail

Butterflies Attracted None known

Nectar Plants for Butterflies

Hamelia patens • Firebush

A robust evergreen shrub or small tree to 10 feet, with bright gray-green leaves. Clusters of reddish-orange tubular flowers are borne on reddish leafstalks.

Native Habitat Hardwood forest margins, coastal hammocks, and shell mounds in Florida, the West Indies, and Central and South America to Paraguay and Bolivia

Hardiness Zones 8 to 11

Blooming Period Year-round in southern Florida; spring to frost in the northern part of the state

Growing Tips Does well in full sun to moderate shade. Prefers some moisture and well-drained soil, but is drought-tolerant once established. Can be used as an understory shrub.

Butterflies Attracted Zebra Heliconian, Monarch, Gulf Fritillary, sulphurs

Helianthus debilis • Beach Sunflower

Depending on the variety, an upright or prostrate spreading herbaceous plant to 4 feet tall or long with heart-shaped leaves. Bears attractive daisy flowers with pale yellow rays (petals) and a ½- to 1-inch-wide purplish brown disk.

Helianthus debilis, **beach sunflower.**

Native Habitat Dunes and beaches from Florida's Atlantic coast to southeast Texas

Hardiness Zones 8 to 11

Blooming Period Year-round in south Florida; spring to frost in the northern part of the state

Growing Tips Prefers full sun and sandy soils. Is extremely drought-tolerant and suffers from overwatering. Beach sunflower is an annual in areas with freezing winter temperatures; it will reseed itself or act as a perennial in central Florida.

Butterflies Attracted Fiery Skipper, Whirlabout Skipper, Checkered White

Monarda punctata • Dotted Horsemint

A 2- to 3-foot-tall perennial with unusual yellow flowers spotted with brown, nestled above pink bracts.

Native Habitat Dry, sandy roadsides or fields and woodland edges from Vermont to Minnesota south to Florida and Texas

Hardiness Zones 4 to 10

Blooming Period Summer to fall

Growing Tips Grow in full sun with some afternoon shade. Drought-tolerant but appreciates good garden soil and some irrigation during dry periods.

Butterflies Attracted Long-Tailed Skipper, Dorantes Skipper, Gulf Fritillary

Salvia coccinea • Tropical Sage, Scarlet Sage

Annual herb 2 to 4 feet tall, with spikes of brilliant scarlet, tubular flowers

Native Habitat Sandy soils and open woods from South Carolina to Florida west along the Gulf coast to Texas and Mexico

Hardiness Zones 8 to 11

Blooming Period Summer to fall

Growing Tips Grow in moist to dry, well-drained soil in sun or part sun. In milder regions, this species is a perennial. Heavy frost will kill the plant, but seeds survive the winter and germinate in spring.

Butterflies Attracted Monarch, Queen, sulphurs, swallowtails, fritillaries

Stachytarpheta jamaicensis Trailing Blue Porterweed

A mounding woolly perennial that grows about 1 foot tall by about 5 feet wide. Blue flowers are borne at the tips of long, stringy spikes at the ends of the stems.

Native Habitat Pinelands and disturbed sites in Florida, and the West Indies

Hardiness Zones 9 to 11

Blooming Period Summer and fall

Growing Tips Plant in a sunny location in any soil. Provide irrigation until established, then only during extended droughts. Will go dormant in colder areas and is not frost-tolerant.

Butterflies Attracted Great Southern White, Cassius Blue, duskywings, sulphurs, Zebra Heliconian, Mangrove and Long-Tailed Skippers

Vernonia gigantea • Ironweed

A perennial with great vertical presence, growing to 7 feet or more when the flattened panicles of purple blooms top the plants in summer and autumn.

Native Habitat Woodland edges and floodplains in Florida

Hardiness Zones 5 to 10

Blooming Period June to October

Growing Tips Plant in sun and moist soil. Prune this hardy, clumping perennial in late spring so it stays bushy and produces more abundant blooms.

Butterflies Attracted Pipevine, Palamedes, and Eastern Tiger Swallowtails

Vernonia gigantea, ironweed.

Midwest

Ann Swengel

My husband, Scott, and I expect a lot from our garden. We want it to serve both birds (nectar for hummingbirds, seeds for small songbirds, nesting and winter cover) and butterflies (caterpillar food plants, nectar sources for adults). We also want the gardens to take care of themselves during the growing season, when we're busy elsewhere conducting field research on birds and butterflies. A wilder, more natural look not only cuts down on maintenance but also provides food and cover for these animals.

But we also scale our expectations realistically to what is possible, both horticulturally and zoologically, on our small city lot. Despite our aspirations to a wilder look, we maintain normal lawn mowing because this is expected in the urban landscape. We grow some garden varieties, such as zinnias, in regular flower beds. Most of our plants, however, are native prairie and sand barrens species of open, sunny habitats, including many great nectar plants.

Most of the garden varieties were here when we moved in, and many of the native flowers were put in by us. But a delightful shaded bed of native wildflowers surprised us, underneath the ferns, our first spring here, and it has been treasured each spring since. These woodland beauties include large-flowered trillium (*Trillium grandiflorum*), Dutchman's breeches (*Dicentra cucullaria*), and the star of the crowd, yellow lady's-slipper (*Cypripedium parviflorum*). While these wildflowers aren't prime butterfly plants, I have noticed that some butterflies, such as Milbert's Tortoiseshells, like to spend time in that part of the yard. In the fall, the butterfly perches on the tall ferns and makes forays into the garden to take nectar from New England asters (*Aster novae-angliae;* now *Symphyotrichum novae-angliae*).

I don't have a large diversity of butterflies because of my urban setting, but I enjoy them anyway. Cabbage Whites and sulphurs (Clouded and Orange) like to cruise

Monarchs, Cabbage Whites, and sulphurs like this one are common even on city lots in the Midwest.

around the yard, hang out around caterpillar food plants (broccoli in the vegetable garden, clover in the lawn), and nectar plants (oregano and other flowers).

Monarchs pass through during migration in late August and September, visiting long-blooming purple coneflower (*Echinacea purpurea*), New England aster, rough blazingstar (*Liatris aspera*), and cup-plant (*Silphium perfoliatum*), a prairie perennial that usually reaches nine feet tall!

I have planted five species of milkweed (*Asclepias syriaca, A. tuberosa, A. incarnata, A. amplexicaulis, A. verticillata*) for larvae of Monarchs and the Milkweed Tiger Moth. American Ladies lay eggs on pussytoes (*Antennaria*). I rarely see Black Swallowtail adults in the yard, but most years I find caterpillars in the garden, usually on carrot leaves, even though other hosts (dill, fennel, parsley) are available.

I deadhead some flowers to prolong the blooming season, leaving others to provide seeds for songbirds. I do not clean my garden in the fall. I leave removal of standing dead vegetation until well into spring, since this is cover for overwintering butterflies in various life stages. I mulch heavily year-round, using mainly wood shavings. I make sure that a good layer is laid down before the ground freezes up.

I've never received negative comments about our "weeds," but I have had many positive comments about our many pretty flowers—they're tall and colorful and different!

Host Plants for Caterpillars

Antennaria plantaginifolia
Plantain-Leafed Pussytoes

Herbaceous perennial 6 inches tall with spoon-shaped leaves and fuzzy white flowers.

Native Habitat Open woods and fields (usually well drained) from the Northeast to Midwest south to Missouri

Hardiness Zones 3 to 9

Blooming Period May

Growing Tips Prefers well-drained soil with partial to full sun. Needs protection from being overrun by taller garden plants. This plant, or one of its relatives, often voluntarily establishes itself in lawns.

Caterpillars Hosted American Lady

Butterflies Attracted American Copper, Eastern Pine Elfin, Juniper Hairstreak

Asclepias tuberosa • Butterfly Weed

Herbaceous perennial 12 to18 inches tall, with thin elongated leaves and orange flower clusters; an excellent accent plant.

Native Habitat Prairies, upland meadows,

eastern U.S. to northern Rockies, Arizona

Hardiness Zones 3 to 9

Blooming Period June to July

Growing Tips Requires partial to full sun in well-drained site. Readily grown from seed. Transplant when young and after all chance of frost is over. Avoid transplanting when older because of its deep, fleshy taproot.

Caterpillars Hosted Monarch

Butterflies Attracted Hairstreaks, fritillaries, Monarch

Aster laevis (Symphyotrichum laevis)
Smooth Aster

Herbaceous perennial that bears pale lavender daisylike flower heads with yellow centers; leaves are narrow and elongated.

Native Habitat Prairies, pine barrens, meadows (usually with average to dry soil); widespread, as far north as Yukon

Hardiness Zones 3 to 9

Blooming Period August to September

Growing Tips Adaptable; prefers average soil moisture in sites with partial to full sun. Easily grown from seed.

Caterpillars Hosted Pearl and Northern Crescents

Butterflies Attracted Painted Lady, Monarch, skippers, sulphurs

Lupinus perennis • Wild Lupine

Herbaceous perennial 1 to 1½ feet tall, spikes with light purple pealike flowers, palmate leaves (in radiating sets of seven to nine leaflets). Plants that flower may die back to the roots by mid- to late summer.

Native Habitat Pine barrens, sand prairies of eastern U.S.

Hardiness Zones 4 to 8

Blooming Period May to June

Growing Tips Requires well-drained sites

Fritillary on *Asclepias tuberosa*, butterfly weed.

'Karner' Melissa Blue on *Lupinus perennis*, wild lupine.

with partial to full sun. Readily grown from seed, but use inoculated or unsterilized soil (legumes require nitrogen-fixing bacteria to establish).

Caterpillars Hosted Clouded and Orange Sulphurs, Gray Hairstreak, Eastern Tailed-Blue, 'Karner' Melissa Blue (rare in gardens), Painted Lady

Butterflies Attracted Monarch, skippers

Viola sororia
Common Blue Violet

Herbaceous perennial 6 to 8 inches tall, with purple butterfly-shaped flowers and heart-shaped leaves that remain green throughout summer.

Native Habitat Damp woods and damp meadows in the East to Midwest

Hardiness Zones 3 to 9

Blooming Period April to May, sometimes September

Growing Tips Prefers average to moist but not soggy soil in shady or sunny sites. May need help so it doesn't get overshadowed and crowded out by taller garden plants. May spring up voluntarily in yard.

Caterpillars Hosted Great Spangled and Aphrodite Fritillaries

Butterflies Attracted None known

Prunus serotina • Black Cherry

Tree with narrow elongated leaves. Small white flowers occur in elongated spikes 4 to 5 inches long, later developing into dark purple berries. Bark becomes scaly on large trees.

Native Habitat Forests, usually with average to moist but not soggy soil; eastern half of U.S.

Hardiness Zones 3 to 8

Blooming Period April to May

Growing Tips Prefers partial to full sun, in fertile but well-drained soil.

Caterpillars Hosted Eastern and Canadian Tiger Swallowtails, Coral and Striped Hairstreaks, Spring Azure, White Admiral, Red-Spotted Purple, Viceroy

Butterflies Attracted Eastern and Canadian Tiger Swallowtails

***Prunus serotina*, black cherry.**

Tiger Swallowtail on *Agastache foeniculum,* anise hyssop.

Nectar Plants for Butterflies

Agastache foeniculum • Anise Hyssop

A hardy prairie perennial 3 to 5 feet tall, with bold blue flower spikes and quilted, anise-scented leaves.

Native Habitat Prairies and woodlands in north-central North America

Hardiness Zones 3 to 8

Blooming Period Midsummer to early autumn

Growing Tips Grow in sun to part sun and moist but well-drained soil. Seed heads remain decorative after flowering ceases.

Butterflies Attracted Many, including Painted Lady, Red Admiral, Monarch, sulphurs

Echinacea pallida
Pale Purple Coneflower

A tough wildflower with stout, nearly leafless stems 2 to 3 feet tall topped by large daisy flower heads with drooping pale rose rays (petals) below coppery brown conelike center disks.

Native Habitat Open woods, savannas, and prairies from Illinois to Iowa south to Arkansas and Oklahoma

Hardiness Zones 3 to 10

Blooming Period Summer

Growing Tips Easily grown in dry or moist, well-drained soil in full sun or part shade. Tolerates drought, heat, humidity, and poor soils.

Butterflies Attracted Swallowtails, fritillaries, Monarch, grass skippers

Heliopsis helianthoides • Oxeye Daisy

An upright, clump-forming perennial growing 3 to 5 feet tall. Produces daisy flower heads 2 to 3 inches in diameter with yellow-orange rays (petals) and brown center disks atop stiff stems. Several cultivars are available.

Native Habitat Rocky woods, thickets, prairies, and along railroad tracks from Quebec to British Columbia, south to Georgia and New Mexico

Hardiness Zones 3 to 9

Blooming Period Summer to early autumn

Growing Tips Easy to grow in average, dry

to moist, well-drained soil in full sun. Tolerates drought and a wide range of soils, including poor ones.

Butterflies Attracted Many, including Monarch, Painted Lady, Red Admiral, skippers

Liatris aspera • **Rough Blazingstar**

A tough and adaptable perennial growing typically 2 to 3 feet tall. Features fluffy, deep rose-purple button-type flower heads crowded on long, terminal flower spikes atop erect, rigid stalks. Blooms somewhat later than most other *Liatris* species.

Native Habitat Dry prairies, woodland openings, and along roadsides and railroad tracks from Michigan to North Dakota south to Oklahoma and Texas

Hardiness Zones 3 to 8

Blooming Period Late summer to fall

Growing Tips Easily grown in average, dry to moist, well-drained soils in full sun. Tolerant of poor soils, drought, and summer heat and humidity but does not thrive in wet winter soils.

Butterflies Attracted Monarch, grass skippers, sulphurs

Monarda fistulosa • **Wild Bergamot**

An adaptable member of the mint family growing 2 to 4 feet tall, with pleasantly pungent foliage. Produces lavender, two-lipped tubular flowers in solitary dense, globular heads that rest on a whorl of pinkish, leafy bracts.

Native Habitat Dry, rocky woods, prairies, roadsides, and along railroad tracks from Quebec to British Columbia south to Georgia and Arizona

Hardiness Zones 3 to 9

Blooming Period Summer

Growing Tips Best grown in dry to moist, well-drained soils in full sun to part sun. Tolerates poor soils and some drought.

Monarda fistulosa, wild bergamot.

Wild bergamot may spread aggressively in the garden.

Butterflies Attracted Swallowtails, fritillaries, Red Admiral, Silver-Spotted Skipper, grass skippers

Phlox pilosa
Prairie Phlox, Downy Phlox

A delicate fibrous-rooted wildflower that grows to 12 inches tall. Loose clusters of tubular, bright pink flowers appear several weeks later than those of creeping phlox, *Phlox stolonifera.* Stems, leaves, and inflorescences are slightly downy.

Native Habitat Open woods, thickets, and prairies, usually in dry soils from Connecticut to Manitoba south to Florida, Texas, and Nebraska

Hardiness Zones 4 to 9

Blooming Period Late spring

Growing Tips Prefers moist to moderately dry, well-drained soils in full sun to light shade. Excellent resistance to powdery mildew.

Butterflies Attracted Grass skippers

Southwest

Jim Brock

The encounter was fleeting. I jumped out of my lounge chair and ran over to get a closer glimpse of the large brown skipper with single hindwing tails. A Brown Longtail! The profusion of cosmos blooms, my garden's main nectar source in late summer, had no doubt garnered the attention of this wanderer from Mexico.

Butterfly gardening in Tucson, Arizona, sometimes rewards me with such rare surprises. Because of our proximity to Mexico and the tropics, we see an amazing diversity of butterflies and hummingbirds, both resident and vagrant. Within just a few years, I have recorded nearly 80 species of butterflies in my yard, including rare vagrants such as the Toltec Roadside Skipper.

My home sits at an elevation of 2,700 feet, about a mile from the base of the Santa Catalina Mountains. The surrounding neighborhood consists of one-acre plots of mostly natural vegetation. There are very few lawns in my area since they are only allowed in backyards. Instead, I have created a butterfly garden. I prefer to plant things close together for a more natural look and to provide more cover for wandering caterpillars and roosting butterflies. Interspersed among the plants are various rocks and boulders that match the natural look of the surrounding area.

Gardening in arid regions of the Southwest presents challenges that can be extreme, with triple-digit summertime heat and extended periods without rain. Drought-tolerant plants native to the Sonoran Desert are well adapted to this harsh climate. Two shrubs that perform well in my garden are kidneywood (*Eysenhardtia orthocarpa*), which has fragrant white blossoms, and bee brush (*Aloysia gratissima*), a lanky but extremely fragrant plant. Both are very attractive to blues, hairstreaks, skippers, and Queens, as well as to native bees and wasps.

In the Southwest, desert pipevine is planted as a host plant for the Pipevine Swallowtail, above.

While it is fun and exciting to see butterflies, I pride myself more by how many different caterpillars complete their life history in my garden. I've included larval food plants that are readily available at nurseries, such as passion-vine (*Passiflora foetida*) for the Gulf Fritillary and desert senna (*Senna covesii*) for the Cloudless Sulphur and Sleepy Orange. Desert hackberry (*Celtis pallida*) was established in my yard when we moved in, hosting a colony of Empress Leilia butterflies.

In addition, I include rarer natives like balloon-vine (*Cardiospermum halicacabum*) for larvae of the Silver-Banded Hairstreak, feather tree (*Lysiloma watsonii*) for the Large Orange Sulphur, and desert pipevine (*Aristolochia watsonii*) for the Pipevine Swallowtail. Most are supplied by our local native plant nurseries. I was rewarded one day by the unusual sight of a Red-Spotted Purple, which strayed into my yard from its typical riparian habitat a mile away, to lay eggs on my Goodding's willow (*Salix gooddingii*).

Growing the plants is one thing, but searching for and finding the caterpillars can be difficult. I know Palmer's Metalmark breeds on my native velvet mesquite (*Prosopis velutina*), but I have yet to find the caterpillars. Some larvae are easily found, including the full-grown Sheep Skipper caterpillar that mysteriously appeared on side-oats grama (*Bouteloua curtipendula*) in my front-yard planter.

A Mexican Yellow caterpillar on *Acacia angustissima*, fern acacia.

Host Plants for Caterpillars

Acacia angustissima
Fern Acacia, White-Ball Acacia

Perennial shrub 2 to 5 feet high, with green bipinnate leaves and creamy marblelike flowers; no thorns. Seed pods are 1 to 3 inches long.

Native Habitat Grasslands, roadsides, and rocky slopes along stream courses in Southwest

Hardiness Zones 8 to 10

Blooming Period May to September

Growing Tips Full sun, drought-tolerant. Good for erosion control.

Caterpillars Hosted Acacia Skipper, Mexican Yellow, Gold-Costa Skipper (rare)

Butterflies Attracted Palmer's and Fatal Metalmarks, Ceraunus and Marine Blues, Texan Crescent

Bouteloua curtipendula
Side-Oats Grama

Grass forms clumps 2 feet high to 1 foot across with 2-foot-high seed stalks and blue-green foliage. Turns brown in winter.

Native Habitat Wide variety of dry-soil habitats such as prairies and rocky hills from the Midwest to California

Hardiness Zones 4 to 9

Blooming Period April to October

Growing Tips Best in full sun; drought-tolerant. May produce volunteers. Can be cut back in late winter to encourage new growth.

Caterpillars Hosted Orange Skipperling, Sheep Skipper

Butterflies Attracted None known (or likely, as plant is wind-pollinated)

Dalea pulchra • Indigo Bush

Perennial shrub, 4 feet high. Foliage grayish green and silvery, leaves small. Rounded, ¾-inch-wide flowers are rose-purple above, whitish below.

Native Habitat Rocky hills and slopes in desert Southwest

Hardiness Zones 8 to 10

Blooming Period Late December to May

Growing Tips Full sun, drought-tolerant; grows in rocky soils.

Caterpillars Hosted Reakirt's Blue, Southern Dogface

Butterflies Attracted Funereal Duskywing, Reakirt's Blue, Arizona Powdered-Skipper

Prosopis velutina • **Velvet Mesquite**

Tree 10 to 20 feet tall, 30 feet wide, with 3-inch-long light yellow fuzzy flowers; compound fernlike leaves 3 to 4 inches long and 1 inch wide, divided into numerous leaflets. Deciduous in winter, although only partially so in warmer areas. Provides much-needed shade.

Prosopis velutina, velvet mesquite.

Native Habitat Watercourses, rocky slopes or grassland flats in Southwest

Hardiness Zones 7 to 10

Blooming Period Mainly April to June, also sporadically later in summer

Growing Tips Full sun, drought-tolerant once established

Caterpillars Hosted Marine Blue, Leda Ministreak (both feed on flowers); Palmer's Metalmark (foliage).

Butterflies Attracted Leda Ministreak

Senna hirsuta var. *glaberrima*, slimpod senna.

Senna hirsuta var. *glaberrima* **Slimpod Senna, Longpod Senna**

Perennial shrub 2 to 3 feet high with waxy green leaves and golden-yellow flowers. Seedpods are 4 to 5 inches long and slender.

Native Habitat Grasslands and roadsides; uplands in Southwest

Hardiness Zones 8 to 10

Blooming Period June to September

Growing Tips Easy to grow in full sun, drought-tolerant.

Caterpillars Hosted Cloudless Sulphur (mostly flowers and buds), Sleepy Orange and Boisduval's Yellow (foliage), Gray Hairstreak (flowers)

Butterflies Attracted None known

Streptanthus carinatus **Twistflower, Arizona Jewel Flower, Silverbell Mustard**

Annual to 1 foot high with blue-green leaves, white flowers, and 2- to 3-inch-long green seedpods.

Native Habitat Desert washes, flats, and slopes in Southwest

Hardiness Zones 8 to 10

Blooming Period January to April

Growing Tips Best in full sun but tolerates partial shade. Reseeds itself.

Caterpillars Hosted Sara and Desert Orangetips, Pearly Marble

Butterflies Attracted None known

Nectar Plants for Butterflies

Aloysia gratissima • Bee Brush, Whitebrush

A perennial shrub usually 8 feet high and 5 feet wide. After rains, produces clouds of vanilla-scented, white verbenalike flowers with yellow throats on 1- to 3-inch spikes. Attractive to bees as well as butterflies.

Native Habitat Slopes, rocky soils, and mesquite bosques in Texas, New Mexico, and Arizona

Hardiness Zones 9 to 11

Blooming Period Spring to fall

Growing Tips Adaptable to various soils in full sun to dappled shade; very drought-tolerant.

Butterflies Attracted American Snout, Queen, Gray Hairstreak

Baccharis salicifolia (*B. glutinosa*) Seep Willow, Mulefat

An erect shrub with woody stems 3 to 10 feet high and willowlike leaves. Produces small, 1/5-inch-diameter, cream-colored flowers in dense clusters at the tips of the branches. *Baccharis* is a dioecious genus; male and female flowers grow on separate plants.

Native Habitat Along watercourses in the desert Southwest, from Texas to California, where it often forms dense thickets

Hardiness Zones 7 to 11

Blooming Period Most of the year, but principally from April to October

Growing Tips Adaptable to various soils; grow in full sun with moderate water.

Butterflies Attracted Great Purple Hairstreak, Gray Hairstreak, American Snout

Dicliptera resupinata • Twin Seed

A perennial subshrub up to 2 feet tall and 4 feet wide, with waxy, bright green foliage and lavender pealike flowers. In autumn, leaves and flower bracts are edged in deep lavender-purple. Dies to the ground in winter.

Native Habitat Open woodlands in New Mexico and Arizona

Hardiness Zones 9 to 11

Blooming Period Spring and fall

Growing Tips Plant in masses as a groundcover. Tolerates sun to partial shade; may not bloom as profusely in heavy shade. Needs a small to moderate amount of water.

Butterflies Attracted Sleepy Orange, Tailed Orange, Mimosa Yellow, Southern Dogface, Mexican Yellow. Host to Texan Crescent caterpillars.

Dicliptera resupinata, twin seed.

Verbena gooddingii, **Goodding's verbena.**

Eysenhardtia orthocarpa • Kidneywood

A delicate shrub or small tree in the pea family growing 8 to 16 feet tall and 12 feet wide. Deciduous, with fragrant gray-green foliage and dense racemes of tiny white spicy-scented flowers.

Native Habitat Rocky slopes and canyons in Arizona

Hardiness Zones 8 to 10

Blooming Period Spring to summer

Growing Tips Prefers full sun and will grow very tall with supplemental water

Butterflies Attracted Great Purple Hairstreak, Marine Blue

Lycium berlandieri • Wolfberry

A spiny shrub to 7 feet tall, with no leaves from spring to fall; remarkable in winter because of its off-season foliage. Also notable for its early blue, lavender, or white tubular, ⅜-inch-long flowers, which cover the bush from February to October and are followed by numerous tomato-red berries.

Native Habitat Open woodlands, grasslands, and desert scrub from Arizona to Texas

Hardiness Zones 8 to 10

Blooming Period Spring through fall

Growing Tips Full sun; grows in rocky soil, and requires little supplemental water.

Butterflies Attracted Arizona Powdered Skipper

Verbena gooddingii (Glandularia gooddingii) • Goodding's Verbena

A short-lived, low-growing, spreading perennial that forms a soft mound 18 inches high and 4 feet wide. Leaves are deeply cut and covered with white hairs. Produces dense spikes to 3 inches long of flattened tubular, lavender-pink flowers at the tips of branches.

Native Habitat Dry slopes, canyons, and mesas to 6,000 feet throughout the Southwest

Hardiness Zones 8 to 10

Blooming Period Spring to summer, then sporadically after rainfall

Growing Tips Grows best in full sun with some supplemental water. Short-lived but self-sows.

Butterflies Attracted Pipevine Swallowtail, Painted Lady

Pacific Coast

Leana Beeman-Sims

Wayward Gardens, our ten-acre nursery on a hilltop just a few ridges in from the northern California coast, is a wild and whimsical place. We have a bit of protection from the southerly wind and coastal fog, and a stunning view of the coast range. In our five years here, we have turned an abandoned horse pasture into a series of lovely gardens, ringed by native oaks, especially coast live oak (*Quercus agrifolia*). The gardens are completely dedicated to providing habitat for wildlife.

The main focus of our nursery is butterflies and hummingbirds, the ravishing beauties of the habitat garden. The first year we attracted hundreds of Monarchs, which came to nectar on Mexican sunflower (*Tithonia rotundifolia*). We were inspired to create a huge, 50-foot-diameter "butterfly spiral." It was planted with Mexican sunflower, milkweeds (*Asclepias*), salvias, and many varieties of annual sunflowers (*Helianthus annuus*), and by late fall it was eight feet tall and exciting to walk into. The Monarchs seem to prefer nectaring at the Mexican sunflowers, and our planting design made it possible to observe them up close.

Our plant collection is based on both larval and nectar plants for butterflies, and berrying and blooming plants for birds. We always have milkweeds, the host plants for Monarch caterpillars. Our favorites are the showy milkweed (*Asclepias speciosa*) and narrow-leafed milkweed (*Asclepias fascicularis*). We like these best because they provide a long season of foliage and thrive in garden conditions, eventually forming large colonies. We also carry Dutchman's pipevine (*Aristolochia californica*), the host for Pipevine Swallowtail larvae, and other important native larval shrubs such as California lilac (*Ceanothus thyrsiflorus*), California buckthorn (*Rhamnus californica* or *Frangula californica*), and California wild rose (*Rosa californica*).

California Sister on *Eschscholzia californica*, California poppy.

We find loads of caterpillars on our plants and often share our enthusiasm with customers. Western Tortoiseshells migrate through our garden in early spring, and we are lucky to find their larvae on *Ceanothus* 'Joan Mirov', one of our favorite California lilac cultivars. Our most recent find was larvae of the Chalcedon Checkerspot on our native honeysuckle (*Lonicera hispidula*).

Open, sunny areas in the middle of the garden are densely planted with flowering annuals and perennials that provide nectar over a long blooming season. We always grow as many sunflowers as we can, as they are enjoyed for three full seasons—by early-spring pollen-loving insects, by butterflies, and by the towhees and sparrows, who devour every last seed in late fall. Popular native perennials for nectaring butterflies include tall verbena (*Verbena hastata*) and coastal aster (*Symphyotrichum chilense*, previously known as *Aster chilensis*), which blooms from spring until fall.

It's a thrill for us to not only observe butterflies and their caterpillars but also watch our customers and friends experiencing butterflies in all their life stages. Children are always especially tickled to see that the Monarch's faces are polka-dotted. We hope that our demonstration gardens will inspire others to change many of their old gardening habits in order to attract and nourish insects, birds, and other garden visitors.

Eriogonum umbellatum, **sulfur buckwheat.**

Host Plants for Caterpillars

Eriogonum umbellatum
Sulfur Buckwheat

Bright yellow flowers, turning red with age, appear above mounding foliage that varies from dark green to whitish silver. A perennial or a subshrub, short-lived but fantastic in bloom.

Native Habitat Dry open rocky slopes in western states

Hardiness Zones 3 to 8

Blooming Period Summer

Growing Tips Prefers dry, sunny locations; extremely drought-tolerant but demands perfect drainage.

Caterpillars Hosted Mormon Metalmark, Bramble Hairstreak, Gray Hairstreak, Square Spotted Blue, Dotted Blue, Acmon Blue, San Bernardino Blue, Green Hairstreak, Gorgon Copper, Purplish Copper, Lupine Blue

Butterflies Attracted Many, including West Coast Lady, Common Buckeye, blues

Holodiscus discolor, **ocean spray.**

Holodiscus discolor
Ocean Spray, Creambush

A fast-growing and graceful deciduous shrub with airy plumes of light pink to white flowers and beguiling crinkly leaves that release a fruity fragrance when crushed. It can reach 20 feet tall.

Native Habitat Moist woodland edges throughout the West

Hardiness Zone 5

Blooming Period Late spring

Growing Tips Benefits from regular pruning to keep it tidy. It needs protection from afternoon sun and likes a bit of summer water.

Caterpillars Hosted Lorquin's Admiral, Pale Swallowtail

Butterflies Attracted Swallowtails

Mimulus aurantiacus (Diplacus aurantiacus) • Sticky Monkey Flower

Attractive foliage and large flowers make this a very appealing subshrub for the butterfly garden. It grows about 4 feet tall

Mimulus aurantiacus, **sticky monkey flower.**

and 6 feet wide. Recent introductions include cultivars that are dark-flowered ('Dark Gulch') and hybrids in a range of colors from white to dark purple.

Native Habitat: It is found on dry, partly shady hillsides from the coast to the Sierra Nevada.

Hardiness Zone 8

Blooming Period Early summer to late fall

Growing Tips Thriving in full sun near the coast, sticky monkey flower needs afternoon shade inland. Very drought-tolerant once established, it also looks good with a bit of supplemental summer water and benefits from occasional pruning.

Caterpillars Hosted Common Buckeye, Chalcedon Checkerspot

Butterflies Attracted Mainly pollinated by bumblebees, sometimes hummingbirds

Quercus agrifolia • Coast Live Oak

Glossy, dark green leaves and light bark make an attractive tree for any western garden. It grows to about 30 feet but can be pruned into a handsome specimen tree

Quercus agrifolia, **coast live oak.**

or even an evergreen hedge. Bark is fire-resistant.

Native Habitat Mixed evergreen forest and valley slopes of Southern California north to Mendocino County

Hardiness Zone 7

Growing Tips Grows quickly and tolerates garden conditions very well.

Caterpillars Hosted California Sister, Boisduval's Hairstreak, Herr's Hairstreak, California Hairstreak, Gray Hairstreak, Goldhunter's Hairstreak, Nut Brown Hairstreak, Santa Monica Mountains

Hairstreak, Echo Blue, Wright's Duskywing, Mournful Duskywing, Propertius Duskywing, Lucustra Duskywing

Butterflies Attracted Early butterflies, such as blues

Alternate Choice *Quercus garryana*, Oregon white oak

Rhamnus californica (Frangula californica) • California Coffeeberry

One of our most beautiful evergreen shrubs, its form is variable. Some are small-leafed and only grow to about 4 feet tall, and others have large leaves and can reach 10 feet.

Native Habitat Coffeeberry is found in full sun near the coast and in the shady understory of mixed hardwood forests inland

Hardiness Zone 7

Blooming Period Spring

Growing Tips Coffeeberry is happy in rich loamy soil with good drainage. The coastal forms thrive with some summer water, and the inland forms are very drought-tolerant, needing no summer water once established.

Caterpillars Hosted Pale Tiger Swallowtail, Gray Hairstreak, Echo Blue

Butterflies Attracted None known, but the nectar is enjoyed by a variety of pollinators, including bumblebees and specialized flies.

Sidalcea malviflora • Checkerbloom

One of our most beautiful coastal wild-flowers, checkerbloom is a perennial with bright pink blooms and glossy dark green foliage. There are two forms, a ground-cover variety and an upright form, much like a miniature hollyhock, that grows to 24 inches high.

Opposite: *Sidalcea malviflora*, checkerbloom.
Right: *Armeria maritima*, seathrift.

Hardiness Zones 8 to 10

Blooming Period Spring through fall

Growing Tips Can take part shade or full sun with regular water; needs well-drained soil.

Caterpillars Hosted Painted Lady, West Coast Lady, Two-Banded Checkered Skipper, Common Checkered Skipper, Gray Hairstreak

Butterflies Attracted Pollinated by bees and wasps

Nectar Plants for Butterflies

Armeria maritima • Seathrift

A mounding plant reaching 6 to 8 inches tall and 10 to 12 inches across, with tidy, grasslike leaves. Produces small, white to rose-pink ballshaped flower heads atop 6- to 10-inch stalks.

Native Habitat Sandy soils or well-drained slopes on sand dunes, coastal grasslands, bluffs, and ridges in California, Oregon, and Washington

Hardiness Zones 6 to 10

Blooming Period Year-round along coast, most profusely in spring elsewhere

Growing Tips Grows best in full sun in well-drained soil, with regular watering in warmer and drier inland areas.

Butterflies Attracted West Coast Lady, skippers, Common Buckeye

Asclepias speciosa • Showy Milkweed

A tough perennial with an upright habit and gray-green leaves with conspicuous veining. Globular umbels, or clusters, to 3 inches across of fragrant pink to light purple starlike flowers are followed by podlike fruits.

Native Habitat Dry slopes, open woodlands, roadsides, and along streams throughout western North America

Hardiness Zones 4 to 9

Blooming Period Late spring and summer

Growing Tips Easy to grow in poor to average, dry to moist soils in full sun. Once established, it is quite drought-tolerant. Spreads by rhizomes to form a clump and may self-seed if pods are not removed before they split open.

Butterflies Attracted Monarch, West Coast Lady

Asclepias speciosa, showy milkweed.

Erigeron glaucus • Seaside Daisy

A low-growing perennial 10 to 12 inches tall and 2 to 3 feet across. Produces 2-inch-wide daisy flower heads with lavender, threadlike rays (petals) and yellow centers.

Native Habitat Coastal bluffs and sand dunes in Oregon and California

Hardiness Zones 9 to 10

Blooming Period Late spring through summer

Growing Tips Prefers well-drained soils and full sun in coastal areas.

Butterflies Attracted West Coast Lady, skippers, Monarch, Common Buckeye, Common Checkered Skipper

Phacelia tanacetifolia • Tansy Phacelia

A hardy annual 12 to 24 inches tall. Fiddleneck-shaped panicles slowly unfurl to reveal blue flowers with white dots at the base of the petals and protruding stamens (male flower parts) that give the flowers a fuzzy look. Attractive to bees as well as butterflies.

Native Habitat A California native of bush scrub and woodland habitats that has naturalized throughout the West

Hardiness Zones 7 to 10

Blooming Period April to July

Growing Tips Easy to grow from seed, blooms in eight weeks. Plant in full to part sun and well-drained soil. Heat-resistant.

Butterflies Attracted Orange Sulphur, West Coast Lady, Common Buckeye

Philadelphus lewisii • Mock Orange

A deciduous, loosely branched, arching shrub to 10 feet tall with flaky bark. Fragrant, showy, white, cup-shaped flowers occur in clusters of 3 to 15 at the ends of branches.

Philadelphus lewisii, mock orange.

Native Habitat Most common in open coniferous forests with moist to dry, rocky soils from southern British Columbia and southwestern Alberta south to California and Montana

Hardiness Zones 5 to 10

Blooming Period May to July

Growing Tips Plant in full to part sun. Drought-tolerant, especially the form native to California.

Butterflies Attracted Swallowtails, sulphurs

Symphyotrichum chilense (*Aster chilensis*) 'Pt. St. George' Coastal Aster

This selection has a very compact form, and grows to about 2 feet high.

Native Habitat Grassy slopes, valley floors, and along streamsides from California to British Columbia

Hardiness Zone 8

Blooming Period Spring through fall

Growing Tips Easygoing and long-blooming, this aster needs room to spread. It likes well-drained soil and does best well mulched.

Butterflies Attracted West Coast Lady, Common Checkered Skipper, Acmon Blue, skippers. Host to Northern Checkerspot and Field Crescent caterpillars.

More Caterpillar Plants for Every Region

Northeast

Agalinis purpurea Purple gerardia
COMMON BUCKEYE

Amorpha fruticosa Leadplant
SILVER-SPOTTED SKIPPER

Anaphalis margaritacea Pearly everlasting
AMERICAN LADY

Asclepias syriaca Common milkweed
MONARCH

Asimina triloba Pawpaw
ZEBRA SWALLOWTAIL

Baptisia tinctoria Wild indigo
SILVER-SPOTTED SKIPPER

Celtis occidentalis Hackberry HACKBERRY
EMPEROR, QUESTION MARK, SNOUT

Juniperis virginiana Eastern Red Cedar
JUNIPER HAIRSTREAK

Laportea canadensis Wood Nettle
RED ADMIRAL, EASTERN COMMA

Prunus species MOURNING CLOAK

Pseudognaphalium obtusifolium Sweet
Everlasting AMERICAN LADY

Sassafras albidum Sassafras
SPICEBUSH SWALLOWTAIL

Viola species Violets GREAT SPANGLED,
VARIEGATED, AND MEADOW FRITILLARIES

Southeast

Amelanchier laevis Allegheny serviceberry
VICEROY, RED-SPOTTED PURPLE

Angelica atropurpurea Angelica
BLACK SWALLOWTAIL

Aquilegia canadensis Eastern wild columbine
SPRING AZURE, COLUMBINE DUSKYWING

Aristolochia serpentaria Virginia snakeroot
PIPEVINE SWALLOWTAIL

Asimina triloba Pawpaw
ZEBRA SWALLOWTAIL

Aster divaricatus (*Eurybia divaricata*)
White wood aster PEARL CRESCENT

Lindera benzoin Spicebush
SPICEBUSH SWALLOWTAIL

Malva sylvestris High mallow
PAINTED LADY, CHECKERED SKIPPER

Myrica cerifera (*Morella cerifera*) Southern
wax myrtle RED-BANDED HAIRSTREAK

Passiflora incarnata Passion-vine
GULF FRITILLARY

Rhododendron canescens Hoary azalea
GRAY COMMA, STRIPED HAIRSTREAK

Sassafras albidum Sassafras
SPICEBUSH SWALLOWTAIL

Zanthoxylum clava-herculis Hercules' club
BLACK SWALLOWTAIL

Florida

Asclepias perennis White swamp milkweed
MONARCH, QUEEN

Asimina reticulata, *A. parviflora*
Pawpaw ZEBRA SWALLOWTAIl

Bacopa monnieri Water hyssop
WHITE PEACOCK

Celtis laevigata Hackberry HACKBERRY AND
TAWNY EMPERORS, SNOUT, QUESTION MARK

Clitoria mariana Butterfly pea
LONG-TAILED SKIPPER

Funastrum clausum White vine
SOLDIER

Galactia regularis Milk pea
CERAUNUS BLUE, GRAY HAIRSTREAK

Lepidium virginicum Pepper grass
GREAT SOUTHERN WHITE, CHECKERED
WHITE

Magnolia virginiana Sweet bay
EASTERN TIGER SWALLOWTAIL

Oxypolis filiformis Water dropwort
EASTERN BLACK SWALLOWTAIL

Parietaria floridana Pellitory
RED ADMIRAL

Salix caroliniana Carolina willow
VICEROY

Zamia pumila Coontie ATALA

Midwest

Andropogon gerardii Big bluestem
WOOD NYMPH, VARIOUS GRASS SKIPPERS

Astragalus canadensis Milk vetch
CLOUDED AND ORANGE SULPHURS,
EASTERN TAILED-BLUE

Celtis occidentalis Hackberry
HACKBERRY EMPEROR, TAWNY EMPEROR

Juniperus virginiana Eastern Red Cedar
JUNIPER HAIRSTREAK

Medicago sativa Alfalfa
CLOUDED AND ORANGE SULPHURS

Pinus banksiana, P. resinosa, P. strobus
Jack, red, eastern white pine
EASTERN PINE ELFIN

Populus tremuloides Quaking aspen
RED-SPOTTED PURPLE, MOURNING CLOAK

Quercus alba, Q. rubra, Q. macrocarpa
White, red, bur oak
BANDED HAIRSTREAK, JUVENAL'S DUSKYWING

Quercus velutina Black oak
JUVENAL'S DUSKYWING

Salix species Willows MOURNING CLOAK,
VICEROY, RED-SPOTTED PURPLE

Trifolium species Clover CLOUDED SULPHUR

Urtica dioica Stinging nettle
EASTERN COMMA, MILBERT'S
TORTOISESHELL, RED ADMIRAL

Southwest

Abutilon palmeri Indian mallow
POWDERED-SKIPPER

Anisacanthus thurberi Desert honeysuckle
ELADA CHECKERSPOT

Aristolochia watsonii Desert pipevine
PIPEVINE SWALLOWTAIL

Celtis pallida Desert Hackberry
AMERICAN SNOUT, EMPRESS LEILIA

Clematis drummondii Virgin's bower
FATAL METALMARK

Dalea frutescens Black dalea
SOUTHERN DOGFACE, REAKIRT'S BLUE

Dicliptera resupinata Twin seed
TEXAN CRESCENT

Fraxinus velutina Arizona velvet ash
TWO-TAILED SWALLOWTAIL

Lysiloma watsonii Feather tree
LARGE ORANGE SULPHUR

*Sarcostemma cynanchoides (Funastrum
cynanchoides)* Vine milkweed QUEEN

Sphaeralcea ambigua Desert mallow
COMMON CHECKERED SKIPPER

Tithonia fruticosa Mexican sunflower
BORDERED PATCH

Pacific Coast

Angelica hendersonii Henderson's angelica
ANISE SWALLOWTAIL

Amorpha californica False indigo
CALIFORNIA DOGFACE, COMMON
HAIRSTREAK, NORTHERN CLOUDYWING

Arabis blepharophylla Rose rock cress
SARA ORANGETIP

Ceanothus incanus Whitethorn
ECHO BLUE, WESTERN TORTOISESHELL

Cornus glabrata Brown dogwood ECHO BLUE

Heteromeles arbutifolia Toyon
ECHO BLUE, GRAY HAIRSTREAK

Penstemon heterophyllus Foothill penstemon
CHALCEDON CHECKERSPOT, COMMON BUCKEYE

Ribes sanguineum Red-flowering currant
ZEPHYR ANGLEWING, TAILED COPPER,
CLOUDY COPPER

Salix exigua Narrowleaf willow
SYLVAN HAIRSTREAK

Scrophularia californica California figwort
CHALCEDON CHECKERSPOT

Sedum spathulifolium Pacific stonecrop
SAN BRUNO ELFIN, DOUDOROFF'S HAIRSTREAK

Sphaeralcea munroana Munro's globemallow
WEST COAST LADY

Symphoricarpos albus Snowberry
COLON CHECKERSPOT

Viola adunca Western dog violet
UNSILVERED FRITILLARY

More Nectar Plants for Every Region

Northeast

Agastache foeniculum Blue giant hyssop

Amorpha fruticosa Leadplant

Anaphalis margaritacea Pearly everlasting

Apocynum androsaemifolium
  Spreading dogbane

Asclepias viridis Green milkweed

Coreopsis tinctoria Tickseed

Helenium autumnale Common sneezeweed

Lindera benzoin Spicebush

Monarda punctata Horsemint

Pseudognaphalium obtusifolium
  Sweet everlasting

Rhododendron arborescens Sweet azalea

Sambucus canadensis American elderberry

Vernonia noveboracensis
  New York ironweed

Southeast

Asclepias tuberosa Butterfly weed

Aster carolinianus (Ampelaster carolinianus)
  Climbing aster

Boltonia asteroides Boltonia

Cephalanthus occidentalis Buttonbush

Clethra alnifolia Sweet pepperbush

Helenium flexuosum Purple-headed
  sneezeweed

Liatris spicata Gayfeather

Lonicera sempervirens Coral honeysuckle

Phlox divaricata Woodland phlox

Pycnanthemum incanum Mountain mint

Solidago caesia Bluestem goldenrod

Stokesia laevis Stokes' aster

*Verbena canadensis (Glandularia
canadensis)* Rose vervain

Vernonia noveboracensis
  New York ironweed

Florida

Bidens alba Spanish needle

Carphephorus corymbosus
  Florida paintbrush

Cephalanthus occidentalis Buttonbush

*Eupatorium coelestinum (Conoclinium
coelestinum)* Mistflower

Glandularia tampensis Tampa vervain

Lachnanthes caroliniana Redroot

Liatris spicata Gayfeather, blazing star

Pontederia cordata Pickerelweed

Serenoa repens Saw palmetto

Midwest

Asclepias incarnata Swamp milkweed

*Aster novae-angliae (Symphyotrichum
novae-angliae)* New England aster

Eupatorium maculatum Joe-pye weed

Eupatorium perfoliatum Boneset

Lespedeza capitata Round-headed
  bush-clover

Liatris pycnostachya Prairie blazingstar

Lithospermum canescens Hoary puccoon

Prunus virginiana Common chokecherry

A Brown Elfin sips nectar on *Vaccinium,* blueberry, a favorite nectar plant in the Northeast.

Pycnanthemum virginianum Mountain mint
Rubus pubescens Dwarf raspberry
Silphium perfoliatum Cup-plant
Solidago nemoralis Gray goldenrod
Vaccinium corymbosum Highbush blueberry

Southwest

Asclepias linaria Pineleaf milkweed
Asclepias subulata Desert milkweed
Baileya multiradiata Desert marigold
Calliandra californica Baja fairy duster
Chrysothamnus nauseosus (*Ericameria nauseosa*) Rabbit brush
Dalea frutescens Black dalea
Encelia farinosa Brittlebush
Eriogonum fasciculatum California buckwheat
Conoclinium dissectum (*Eupatorium greggii*) Gregg's mistflower
Mimosa biuncifera Wait-a-minute bush
Sapindus drummondii Western soapberry

Pacific Coast

Achillea millefolium Yarrow
Aesculus californica California buckeye
Cirsium occidentale Cobweb thistle
Eriogonum latifolium Coastal buckwheat
Gilia capitata Blue-headed gilia
Grindelia stricta Gumweed
Helianthus californicus California sunflower
Monardella villosa Coyote mint
Rudbeckia californica California coneflower
Salvia sonomensis Sonoma sage
Sedum spathulifolium Pacific stonecrop
Stachys chamissonis var. *cooleyae* Cooley's hedge nettle
Solidago californica California goldenrod
Trichostema lanatum Woolly blue-curls

USDA Hardiness Zone Map

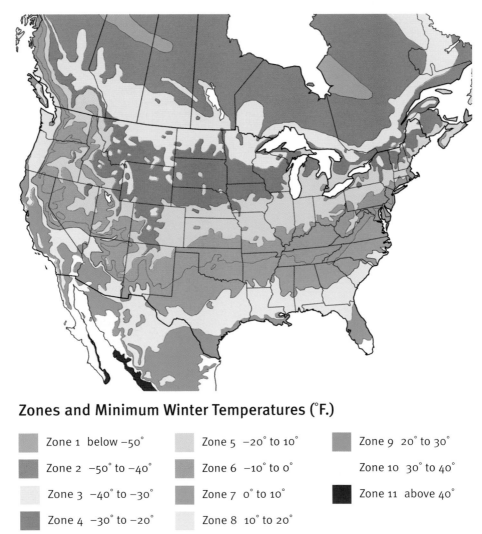

Zones and Minimum Winter Temperatures (°F.)

Zone 1 below −50°

Zone 2 −50° to −40°

Zone 3 −40° to −30°

Zone 4 −30° to −20°

Zone 5 −20° to 10°

Zone 6 −10° to 0°

Zone 7 0° to 10°

Zone 8 10° to 20°

Zone 9 20° to 30°

Zone 10 30° to 40°

Zone 11 above 40°

For More Information

Butterfly Gardening
Xerces Society and Smithsonian Institution
Sierra Club Books, 1998

Butterfly Gardens
Alcinda Lewis, editor
Brooklyn Botanic Garden, 1995

Handbook for Butterfly Watchers
Robert Michael Pyle
Houghton Mifflin Company, 1992

How to Spot Butterflies
Patricia Taylor Sutton and Clay Sutton
Houghton Mifflin Company, 1999

Stokes Beginner's Guide to Butterflies
Donald and Lillian Stokes, Mary Tondorf-
Dick (editor)
Little, Brown and Company, 2001

BUTTERFLY BOOKS FOR CHILDREN
Becoming Butterflies
Anne Rockwell and Megan Halsey
Walker & Company, 2002

Butterflies in the Garden
Carol Lerner
HarperCollins, 2002

BUTTERFLY GUIDEBOOKS
Butterflies through Binoculars
(Regional guides for the East, West,
Florida, and the Boston–New
York–Washington area)
Jeffrey Glassberg
Oxford University Press

**Field Guide to North American
Butterflies**
National Audubon Society
Alfred A. Knopf, Inc., 1997

**Peterson Field Guide to Eastern
Butterflies**
Paul A. Opler
Houghton Mifflin Company, 1998

**Peterson Field Guide to Western
Butterflies**
Paul A. Opler
Houghton Mifflin Company, 1999

**Peterson First Guide to Caterpillars of
North America**
Amy Bartlett Wright, Roger Tory Peterson
Houghton Mifflin Company, 1998

There are many excellent regional guidebooks. Consult your local bookstore or nature center.

Organizations and Nurseries

Journey North
An educational website that engages children in the study of wildlife migration worldwide.
www.learner.org/jnorth

The Lepidopterists' Society
c/o Natural History Museum of Los Angeles
900 Exposition Boulevard
Los Angeles, CA 94007
www.lepsoc.org

Monarch Watch
University of Kansas
Entomology Program
1200 Sunnyside Avenue
Lawrence, KS 66045
www.monarchwatch.org

North American Butterfly Association
4 Delaware Road
Morristown, NJ 07960
www.naba.org

Xerces Society
4828 SE Hawthorne Boulevard
Portland, OR 97215
www.xerces.org

Association of Florida Native Nurseries
P.O. Box 434
Melrose, FL 32666
877-352-2366
www.afnn.org

Gardens North
5984 Third Line Road North, RR#3
North Gower, ON K0A 2T0 Canada
613-489-0065
www.gardensnorth.com

Goodwin Creek Gardens
P.O. Box 83
Williams, OR 97544
800-846-7359
www.goodwincreekgardens.com

Niche Gardens
1111 Dawson Road
Chapel Hill, NC 27516
919-967-0078
www.nichegardens.com

Perennial Pleasures Nursery
P.O. Box 147
East Hardwick, VT 05836
802-472-5104
www.perennialpleasures.net

Plants of the Southwest
3095 Agua Fria Road
Santa Fe, NM 87507
505-438-8888
www.plantsofthesouthwest.com

Prairie Nursery
P.O. Box 306
Westfield, WI 53964
800-476-9453
www.prairienursery.com

Las Pilitas Nursery
8331 Nelson Way
Escondido, CA 92026
760-749-5930; and
3232 Las Pilitas Road
Santa Margarita, CA 93453
805-438-5992
www.laspilitas.com

Contributors

Jim and Dotti Becker operate Goodwin Creek Gardens in Williams, Oregon, where they grow herbs, fragrant plants, native American species, and plants that attract hummingbirds and butterflies. They are also coauthors of *An Everlasting Garden* and *Scented Geraniums*.

Leana Sims is a Sebastopol, California–based master gardener specializing in native plants. Active in native plant and butterfly groups, she writes and lectures on habitat gardening when she is not tending to her nursery business, Hummingbird Hill.

Jim Brock, coauthor of *Butterflies of Southeastern Arizona, Butterflies of North America,* and *Caterpillars in the Field and Garden: A Field Guide to the Butterfly Caterpillars of North America*, lives in Tucson, Arizona, and studies the life histories of butterflies in the Southwest and northern Mexico.

Claire Hagen Dole, guest editor, is the former publisher of *Butterfly Gardeners' Quarterly*. She writes on wildlife gardening for numerous publications and for her website, www.butterflygardeners.com. She lives in Seattle, Washington.

Eric Eaton is a writer, illustrator, and naturalist with a particular interest in entomology. His most recent book, cowritten with Kenn Kaufman, is *Kaufman Field Guide to Insects of North America* (2007). He lives in Tucson, Arizona.

Kim Hawks is the founder and former owner of Niche Gardens, a native-plant nursery in Chapel Hill, North Carolina. She writes and lectures widely on native plants and garden design.

Bernard S. Jackson is the former curator of the Memorial University Botanical Garden in St. John's, Newfoundland. The author of *Mindful of Butterflies*, he lives in Truro, Nova Scotia.

Sharon Lovejoy is an author and illustrator whose books include *Country Living Gardener: A Blessing of Toads; Trowel & Error; Sunflower Houses; Roots, Shoots, Buckets & Boots*; and *Hollyhock Days*. She is also a contributing editor for *Country Living Gardener*, with the award-winning feature column, "Heart's Ease." She is a part-time resident of Cambria, California, and South Bristol, Maine.

Jane Ruffin is a naturalist and photographer who lectures widely on butterflies. As an associate of the Academy of Natural Sciences in Philadelphia, she has been on three scientific expeditions to Africa. She lives in Pennsylvania.

Phil Schappert studies butterfly-plant interactions and teaches ecology at the University of Texas at Austin. He and his wife, Pat, manage the Stengl "Lost Pines" Biology Station near Smithville, Texas. He is the author of *A World for Butterflies: Their Lives, Behavior, and Future*.

Pat and Clay Sutton are writers, lecturers, and naturalists who have cowritten several books, including *How to Spot Butterflies, How to Spot an Owl,* and *How to Spot Hawks and Eagles*. Both are active at the New Jersey Audubon Society's Cape May Bird Observatory, and Pat is also a board member of the North American Butterfly Association. They live near Cape May, New Jersey.

Ann Swengel is a Wisconsin-based naturalist, writer, and population biologist who researches prairie butterflies. An active member of the North American Butterfly Association, she has served as its vice president and edited the results of international butterfly counts.

Pamela F. Traas is a freelance writer, photographer, and former newspaper columnist. The author of *Gardening for Florida's Butterflies*, she lives in Safety Harbor, Florida.

Illustrations
Steve Buchanan

Photos

Neil Soderstrom cover, pages 63, 85, 91

David Cavagnaro pages 4, 33, 35, 38, 40, 52, 54 both, 55, 60, 71, 75, 76, 77, 78, 79 both, 87, 88, 89 bottom, 95 left, 97, 99, 100 bottom, 101 both, 102

Rick & Nora Bowers pages 24, 25, 26 both, 27 both, 28, 42 all, 43, 44 top, 69, 93

Jane Ruffin pages 31, 32, 36, 39, 48, 50 inset, 59, 90, 109

Alan & Linda Detrick pages 44 bottom, 53, 70, 72 top, 81

Jim Brock pages 46, 94, 95 right, 96

Bernard S. Jackson page 50 top

Jerry Pavia pages 56, 72 bottom, 100 top, 103, 104, 105

Jim Becker page 58

Sharon Lovejoy page 64

Pat & Clay Sutton page 73

Pamela F. Traas pages 82, 83, 84

Ann Swengel page 89 top

Index

PROVIDING EXPERT GARDENING ADVICE FOR OVER 60 YEARS

Join Brooklyn Botanic Garden as an annual Subscriber Member and receive our next three gardening handbooks delivered directly to you, plus *Plants & Gardens News*, *BBG Members News*, and reciprocal privileges at many botanic gardens across the country. Visit www.bbg.org/subscribe for details.

BROOKLYN BOTANIC GARDEN ALL-REGION GUIDES

World renowned for pioneering gardening information, Brooklyn Botanic Garden's award-winning guides provide practical advice in a compact format for gardeners in every region of North America. To order other fine titles, call 718-623-7286 or shop online at shop.bbg.org. For additional information about Brooklyn Botanic Garden, call 718-623-7200 or visit www.bbg.org.